The Vietnamese Culinary Culture

THE VIETNAMESE CULINARY CULTURE

Research: Lạp Chúc Nguyễn Huy & Xuân Tàm
Editing and Translation : Vinh-The Lam
Cover Design: Uyên Nguyên Trần Triết
Layout: Công Nguyễn
Published by Nhân Ảnh 2023
ISBN: 9798869388834

Copyright@LapChucNguyenHuy

The Vietnamese Culinary Culture

LẠP CHÚC NGUYỄN HUY

With the Collaboration of
XUÂN TÀM

Edited and Translated Into English by
VINH-THE LAM

NHÂN ẢNH 2024

CONTENTS

Introduction	9
Part 1. Royal Meal	13
1. Royal meal	15
2. Yin and yang	25
3. Identification of the food chi	33
4. The chi of flavors	39
Part 2. Practical Use of Culinary Culure	49
5. Chi of internal organs	51
6. Use of food chi	63
Part 3. Culinary Culture in Spiritual Life	73
7. Worshipped meal	77
Part 4. Culinary Culture and Religion	93
8. Vegetarian meal	95
Appendix 1. Chi in fruit	115
Appendix 2. Culture in meals	119
Appendix 3. Additives	129
Appendix 4. Palace feasts under Nguyễn Dynasty	139
Appendix 5. Vegetables in Vietnamese poetry	147
Bibliography	**159**

INTRODUCTION

On September 12-13, 2019, the meeting of UNESCO held in Italy discussed the two issues of culture and culinary art. According to UNESCO, within each nation, the traditional culinary art, relating to food selection and preparation to make delicious dishes, has created the tangible and intangible cultural heritages, symbolizing the cultural identity and pride of each nation. Today, the local culinary culture has crossed the national and even continental frontier to become the passage connecting the cultures of all nations. Therefore, Mr. Ernesto Ottone, Deputy Director-General of UNESCO, has said: **«*Investing in cultural heritage and culinary art linked with culture have reinforced the developments of both economy and social safety and helped the UNESCO's program reach its objectives in 2030.*[1]»** Especially now with the expansion of world tourism, the culinary culture is at the same time a factor in attracting tourists with all kinds of delicious foods and a door opening to the culture of a nation which is being visited for cultural discovery. So, what culinary culture really is?

The culinary culture is a system of symbols of customs and tastes of a people that helps them identify their members through their ways of eating-drinking, a part of their own cultural identity.

The culinary culture of a people is identified through:

• *The methods of cooking, preparing, presenting the dishes in accordance with tradition, customs to offer special dishes symbolizing the cultural identity of the people,*

• The table manners of people during the eating of meals,
• The respect for habits, customs, and taboos while eating,
• Beliefs, religions, for example, offering meals in accordance with ancestors worshipping, vegetarian meals of Caodaist and Buddhist followers.

Culture is the accumulation of spiritual values from generations to generations, resulting in the creation of:

• The soul of each nation,
• The standards for the relationships between the people and between the people and the society.

In its way of development, the culture is characterized by **its continuity, its heredity, and its permanence.** Its heredity means that the Vietnamese culture while keeping things handed down from our ancestors (and thus, being called traditional) still accepts good and progressive things from other cultures.

In the culinary culture, what did the Vietnamese people inherit from their ancestors? In addition to the dishes (tangible cultural heritage), we also have inherited three kinds of meals symbolizing the intangible cultural heritage:

•*The yin-yang culinary art through the royal meal,*

•*The worshipped meal offered to our ancestors and to the deities symbolizing the culinary art in our folk religion,*

•*The vegetarian meal symbolizing the Buddhist and Caodaist religious culture.*

In the past, when the western nutrition science[1] has not yet exercised any influence on it, the culinary aspect of the Far

---

[1] The western nutrition science pays special attention to the volumes of calories needed for for each person, and to the calculation of them for protids, lipids, glucids, vitamins, minerals, fibers (celluose), in comparison with calcium, phosphorus, magnesium, iodine, sodium, and potassium, etc.

Eastern culture[2] was heavily inheriting those three above-mentioned kinds of meals symbolizing the intangible cultural heritage. Today, although the yin-yang culinary art is quite fairly felt in the culinary life of the Vietnamese people but the worshipped meals offered to the ancestors and the deities still exist like in the old days in the intangible part of the Vietnamese culinary culture, and that forms the contents of this book presented in 4 parts:

- Part 1. The Royal Meal symbolizing the culinary culture of the folk people

First of all, understanding the culinary culture in the Royal Meal (Chapter 1) then guiding the readers in the following topics:

- *Identification of yin-yang (Chapter 2)*
- *Feeling the yin-yang in the daily meals (Chapter 3)*
- *The Chi of flavors in foods (Chapter 4)*

- Part 2. Application of yin-yang in culinary art

Through the experience of yin-yang stabilization by Xuân Tàm, we will understand how to prevent diseases caused by the yin-yang in foods (Chapters 5, 6)

- Part 3. The worshipped meals symbolizing the culinary culture in the folk religion, and the answer to the question why the dishes of an ordinary daily meal become sacred when offered to the deities (Chapter 7)

- Part 4. The religious vegetarian meal as means of leading the souls of the Buddhist and Caodaist followers after their deaths (Chapter 8)

Finally, the author hopes to receive ideas, criticisms from the readers so that the book could be improved in its next edition.

---

[2] The Far Eastern cultural zone includes China, Japan, Vietnam, Korea ...

Part 1

ROYAL MEAL
Symbol of the folk people's culinary culture

The culture is the soul of a nation created by its own people to serve as standards for the behavior in all activities of the society, including the royal culinary culture playing as norm for the people to follow. In order to understand the culinary culture of the people, therefore, we may try to understand the royal meal of the Nguyễn emperors of the old days.

Today, the influence of the royal meal is no longer deep like in the past but it still can be fairly felt in the people's culinary culture, just like we often tell each other:

• *When you eat cooked duck meat don't forget to have it dipped in gingered fish sauce (meaning to have a balanced combination of the cold yin chi of duck meat and the hot yang chi of ginger)*
• *When seeing that her grandchildren eat a lot of durians, longan, the grandmother, having experience in culinary culture, will say: "Be careful You'll be getting hot" (meaning that these*

two kinds of fruit are very yang-wise, i.e., containing much hot yang chi; eating too much of them will worsen those internal diseases caused by hot yang chi such as hemorrhoids, loss of sleep…).

When we try to understand the royal meal, we will encounter several instances of the influence of this above-mentioned food chi. After the lesson on the royal meal, therefore, together we will try to understand the following things:

• *The method of identifying the Yin-Yang chi in foods,*
• *The hot or cold chi in internal body organs,*
• *Organizing the dishes into "prescriptions" having the capability to balance the Yin-Yang chi for disease prevention.*

1

Royal Meal
(Ngự thiện)

In Sino-Vietnamese, the Royal Meal is called «*Ngự Thiện*» (御 ngự: relating to the king, 善 thiện: the meal). In the Royal Meal, we see:

• *The tangible culture through the culinary art of the highly talented royal cooking team and through the grouping of all kinds of delicious foods offered to the king by the people from all over the country.*
• *The intangible aspect of the Vietnamese culinary culture exercised by the royal physicians, making the royal meal turn into some kind of prescription for disease prevention by achieving the yin-yang balance between the foods and the chi of the king's internal organs.*

1. Organization of the Royal Meal

The preparation of the royal meal was taken care of by the cook team called Nội Trù thuyền (in 1802), and then Tư Thiện đội (1808) and finally Thượng Thiện đội under the reign of Emperor Minh Mạng[3]. In 1886, Dr. Hocquard[4] was allowed to visit the royal palace including the royal kitchen manned by a large group of 100

---
[3] Working next to the đội Thượng Thiện there were:
- viện Thượng Trà responsible for provision of beverages for the emperor,
- Đội Phụng Thiện lresponsible for the meals of the Queen Mother, residing at Từ Thọ (Diên Thọ) Palace,
- Ty Lý thiện responsible for feasts, death anniversary meals of the royal family.
[4] Charles Edouard Hocquard, *Une campagne au Tonkin*, Arlea, pp. 605-607.

royal cooks. «*Everyday, each person received 30 quan and went to market to buy foods needed to prepare one dish... In addition to the cooking team, there were 500 persons responsible for hunting the animals, 50 persons for shooting the birds, 50 persons for fishing, 50 persons for getting the swallow's nests, 50 persons for preparing tea*[5]*...*»

Under the Nguyễn Dynasty, the term used to describe the meal eating of the emperor was *"Ngài ngự thiện"* and the one describing the royal meal was *"Ngự Thiện,"* (御 ngự: of the king; 膳 thiện: meal) which consisted of 35 courses[5] called "Phẩm Vị" (品 phẩm: meal; 味 vị: taste) prepared by the Thượng Thiện đội (上 thượng: above, top; 膳 thiện: meal), which included 50 members, each one specializing in one kind of dish. When the meal's preparation is done, and after having heard the bell ring, the chef team put everything into the ornate crimson gold-plated covered trays and delivered them to the royal guards. The royal guards would transfer these trays to the eunuchs, who, in turn, transferred them to the ladies-in-waiting, who served meal to the emperor.

When the emperor sat down for his meal, all bowls, plates, chopsticks must be well placed, even the piece of fried fish, or the rounds of ground pork sausage must be squarely cut. Except for Emperors Duy Tân and Bảo Đại, the emperor always ate meal by himself. Sometimes, a mandarin could be assigned to be there to maintain a conversation with the emperor; this situation was called *"chầu thiện."* Some other times, a mandarin could be assigned to have meal with the emperor but on a separate table; this situation was called *"ban thiện."*

---

[5] In 1886, Hocquard and Baille were allowed to visit the royal palace but reported different statistics since they were guided by two different persons.

2. Tangible Culture: Food Ingredients

In addition to the ingredients ued to prepare the dishes for the Royal Meal, such as all kinds of special sea foods, swallow nests, shark fins, deer tendons, abalones, we have to mention all kinds of special foods offered to the emperor by the people from all over the country[6]. Today, these royally-offered special foods can still be found in some regions, for example:

- **Animals**

Đông Tảo chickens *(Đông Cảo),* also called royally-offered chickens, were special products of the village of Đông Tảo, district of Khoái Châu, province of Hưng Yên, with their feet having big scales (dragon scales) to prepare special dishes.

Nine-spurred roosters were offered to the king since the Hùng Vương era (according to the legend). The village of Xuân Sơn of the mountainous area, district of Tân Sơn, province of Phú Thọ was believed to be the original birthplace of these nine-spurred roosters[7] in the legend of Sơn Tinh (Mountain God) - Thuỷ Tinh (Water God).

Fulica Atra *(Sâm Cầm),* a kind of migrating birds, of the Rallidae family, from the West Lake area, Hà Nội, was considered as a special product offered to the king, and, thus, we had this saying: *«Cá rô Đầm Sét*[8] *(Anabas of Đầm Sét), sâm cầm Hồ Tây* (Fulica Atra of West Lake).»

Semilabeo Notabilis *(Cá Anh Vũ),* was a special kind of fish that had thick-cartilage lips that could suck on the rocks, and that only

---

[6] In 2008, based on historical documents, the Centre for the Preservation of Historical Vestiges of the Ancient Capital City of Huế recreated the ceremony of tribute of loquat, which included the following steps:
- Ceremony of announcement at Lương Quán community hall,
- Ceremony of procession from Lương Quán community hall to Phủ dock on the bank of Hương River (7 boats carrying people with the tribute fruit, and 1 boat carrying the organizing committee),
- Ceremony of reception at Ngọ Môn Gate including the following smaller ceremonies: ceremony of incense offering, ceremony of alcohol offering, ceremony of fruit offering, ceremony of fruit accepting, and ceremony of Minh biểu thành tâm (responding ceremony with warm heart)
[7] Nine-spurred roosters were mentioned in the legend Sơn Tinh – Thủy Tinh as a gift requested by Hùng Vương in Mỵ Nương's wedding, together with nine-tusked elephants, and nine-red haired horses.
[8] Anabas of Đầm Sét, village of Xuân Thiên, district of Thọ Xuân, province of Thanh Hóa was also among the special products used to be tributes to the king.

ate algae in places having strong currents. The home ground of Anh vũ fish was the upper basin of Red River, Kỳ Cùng River, Lam River (provinces of Yên Bái, Phú Thọ, Hòa Bình, Lạng Sơn). According to the legend, the custom of offering tributes to the king has existed since the Hùng Vương era.

Fulica Atra   *Semilabeo Natobilis*

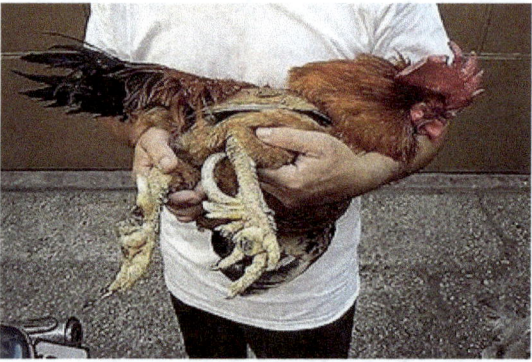

Đông Tảo Chickens   *Nine-spurred Rooster of Phú Thọ*

- **Vegetables and fruit**

Hạc Trì persimmons, originally from the village of Bạch Hạc (City of Việt Trì, province of Phú Thọ).

Longan of phố Hiến (Province of Hưng Yên), well-known from the 16th century.

Rice flakes of the village of Vòng, a special product used as food tribute to the king; Vòng village is about 5-6 km from downtown Hà Nội, currently, ward of Dịch Vọng, district of Cầu Giấy, Hà Nội.

Tribute banana from province of Nam Định, thus, people used to say: «*Đọc thơ Tú Xương ăn chuối ngự* » (Reading Tú Xương's poems while eating tribute banana).

Kim Tân sugar cane, from province of Thanh Hóa, long-time well-known food tribute to the king every year.

Mango of Đá Trắng Pagoda, province of Phú Yên, the mango tree is now over 200-year old.

Thiều Lychee, from Lục Ngạn, province of Bắc Giang.

Tribute Banana of Nam Định   Longan of Hưng Yên   Hạc Trì Persimmons of Phù Thọ   Kim Tân Sugar Cane of Thanh Hóa

▪ Rice

De Rice from An Cựu (Huế), Tám Xoan Rice from Hải Hậu (Nam Định). The cooked rice was prepared with *Ngự Túc rice* (御 ngự: of the king; 粟 túc: rice), provided by the Ministry of Public Works, usually the rice called "gạo de" grown in the fields of An Cựu[9] located inside the capital city of Huế.

The volume of rice eaten by the emperor everyday was weighted very accurately. When the emperor did not have appetite, the Royal Physician was called in and prepared some medication, which he tested right in front of the emperor before he did take by the emperor. The rice for the emperor's meal must be very white and each grain was carefully selected; after the cooking is done, the cooking pot was destroyed.

---

[9] Tôm càng bóc vỏ bỏ đuôi, (With shell-less and tailless tiger shrimps), Gạo de An Cựu em nuôi mẹ già. (and with An Cựu "de" rice, I nourish my old mother.). Kim Luông tươi tốt vườn chè, (The tea plantations in Kim Luông are all green and nice,) Gạo de An Cựu, đĩa muối mè cũng theo nhau. (With An Cựu "de" rice, despite of only a dish of salt and sesame as food, we'll stay together.).

- **Water**

The water used in the food cooking in the imperial palace was taken from the Hàm Long wells of Bảo Quốc Pagoda, or from the Cam Lồ wells at the foot of Thủy Vân Mountain, or from the upper basin of Hương River. The emperor only drank the water that had already been carefully steamed or some kind of alcohol made of well-spiced lotus nuts.

5. Intangible Culture in the Royal Meal

The characterization of the culinary culture of the Royal Meal is also based on the concept of culture of UNESCO, which includes the two following parts:

- *The tangible culture is expressed in the most special foods of the country offered to the emperor, and the most delicious dishes prepared by the talented royal chef team.*
- *The intangible culture is the organization of he Royal Meal based on the two invisible factors : the **yin chi and yang chi** in the foods.*

In the old days, just like the peoples of other countries in the Far Eastern cultural zone, the Vietnamese people's behaviour was based on the science of observation, for example, in the culinary art, they observed that some foods (e.g., cinnamon, ginger, alcohol…) created heat in the body and called them yang foods, and for the other foods, creating some coldness in the body, they called them yin foods.[10] Based on this knowledge from the

---

[10] The observation of the yin chi and the yang chi originated from the I Ching. About 5,000 years ago, the wise men observed phenomena in the universe and discovered that there were chi phenomena going down from the sky to the earth, such as light, wind … and there were also chi phenomena going up from the earth to the sky like steam. These two chi phenomena flowing up and down without interruption and created all the visible physical phenomena of the world. The wise men drew an unbroken bar ▬▬▬ to symbolize the yang chi going down from the sky, and a broken bar ▬▬ ▬▬ to symbolize the yin chi going up from the earth. The two yin and yang bars interacted and created all the phenomena that we could observe in the universe. And from these two yin and yang bars the wise men have written the I Ching, which, without any word, expressed the life process of men in the great universe. At the present, in order to understand the invisible part, i e., the chi, of foods, we must apply the method used by people in the old days in understanding yin-yang, and that is **OBSERVE** and **FEEL**.

observatiion of the yin chi (fresh, cold) and yang chi (warm, hot) of foods, handed down for thousand years within the Far Eastern culture zone, the Đội Thượng Thiện (Royal Chef Team) and the mandarins called Thái Y (Royal Physicians) organized the Royal Meal with nutrition and disease prevention in mind. In the royal palace, therefore, the culinary art was not solely the sophisticated preparation of the Royal Meal from selected precious and delicious foods but the most important thing of the meal was that each dish needed to be considered as a medication to balance the yin chi and yang chi.

■ **Prescription-meal**

Each Royal Meal is a «prescription» aimed at preserving health, preventing or treating disease for the emperor by keeping the yin-yang balance between the foods and between the foods with the emperor's potential chi (cold or hot). This duty was carried out by:

- *The Royal Chef Team should pay attention to several "taboos" in order to guarantee the safety of the emperor's eating and drinking, and would be placed under the control of the Institute of Royal Physicians,*[11]
- *The Institute of Royal Physicians*[12] *was responsible for organizing the dishes of each meal to become a « prescription» for both nutrition and disease prevention.*

---

[11] In the afternoon of April 26, 2018, in the garden of Thiệu Phương – Imperial Palace, Huế, the exhibition "Thái Y Viện triều Nguyễn" (i.e., Institute of Royal Physicians of the Nguyễn Dynasty) introduced almost 50 copies of the royal records (Châu bản, Mộc bản) of the Nguyễn Dynasty, providing valuable information about the Institute of Royal Physicians of the Nguyễn Dynasty.

[12] Prevention measures and punlishments: "Making mistakes in the preparation of drugs for the emperor, making mistakes in markting the package of drugs, the responsible physician will be subject to *100 strokes; inappropriate using of selected drugs will be subject to 60 strokes. Using forbidden foods in preparing the royal meal, the responsible chef will be subject to 100 strokes. For unclean foods, the punishment will be 80 strokes, making mistakes in selecting appropriate foods will be subject to 60 strokes. After having prepared the foods or drugs, forgetting to test them will be subject to 50 whips;* the mandrins called «giám lâm, đề điệu » will receive punishments that were two levels below the ones received by the chef or the physician. If these mandrins and the chef brought these ingredients by mistake to the place where the royal meal was prepared, they will be subject to 100 strokes, and will be forced to drink them.

This disease treating method by balancing the yin-yang chi was almost **unchanged** from the past to the present, i.e., what the Royal Physicians of the old days did were exactly the same practices of the oriental-medicine doctors of today Its basic principle is following the yin-yang theory: *the chi of foods must be balanced with one another, and with the chi* (cold, hot) *of the consumers' internal organs.*

In order to turn the Royal Meal into a «prescripion,» in addition to their knowledge of medicine-pharmacy, the Royal Physicians must also understand very clearly the following things:

1) Identification of the yang foods and the yin foods:

The yang foods creating heat like cinnamon, ginger, pepper, longan, lychee, mango, jackfruit, pineapple; the yin foods having cold chi like abalone, jellyfish, sea cucumber, turtle, shrimp, fish… With this knowledge, the Royal Physicians will:

Balance the yin-yang chi in the foods. For example: Longan sweet soup (lotus nuts stuffed in longans, both of them having yang chi), abalone, duck meat (yin chi) dipped into ginger fish sauce (high yang chi).

Balance the food chi with the weather of each season. In summer, when the temperature was very high, a royal meal prepared with yang foods like red pepper, black pepper, ginger, goat meat, alcohol … would cause more heat in the emperor's body and make him feeling uneasy and losing sleep. Therefore, in summer the royal chefs must offer the emperor fresh, cold foods like vegetables or fruit, or lotus nut sweet soup…

2. Understanding the chi of the emperor's internal organ

The human body possesses two principal states of the chi that we need to know: the hot chi state and the cold chi state.

> • *The hot chi state makes the skin reddened, lips cracked, nose bleeding, sweating; internally there are symptoms of yin chi exhaustion like constipation, thirsty,*
> • *The cold chi state is expressed by ageing, too much sex, leasing to serious diseases.*

From the observation of the chi state of the emperor (cold or hot), knowing which internal organ is weakened, the Royal Physician will select beforehand which meal ingredients (yin or yang) to make the "prescription-meal" appropriate for the emperor's chi state, and for the cold or hot weather of the time… For example:

If already having hot chi state with symptoms like swollen and reddened lips and tongue, constipation, loss of sleep, nose bleeding, hemorrhoids, red pimples, pustule acne … and the emperor continued to eat and drink hot foods like alcohol, cinnamon, mango, longan these diseases would worsen. The Royal Physician, therefore, had to select yin foods like green vegetables, fresh fruit, and stop or lessen usage of yang foods and spices like pepper (both red and black) and alcohol …

If having observed that the emperor has the cold chi state caused by the kidney chi being weakened by ageing or by excessive sexual activities, the Royal Physician would improve the emperor's kidney chi state by giving him ginseng drink, medicated alcohol, warm water, but with just enough quantities appropriate for his body.

It is the author's hope that the culinary culture of the Royal Meal would make us think again after we had seen our family doctors, and had good results in the blood, uninary, feces tests, and had properly nutritional meals in accordance with our doctors' advices but still had this or that disease symtom. If that happens, do not just think that «I've eaten well in accordance with the nutrition science, and I've regularly rexercised in accordane with my doctor's advice.» You've got to think about the yin-yang chi in your daily meals and try to understand specifically the yin-yang chi in your foods (Chapters 2, 3, and 4), and the issue of your internal organs' chi (Chapter 5).

2

Yin and Yang

The Western nutritional method pays much attention to the numbers of calories,[13] the lipids, the glucids, the proteins, and all kinds of vitamins ... but not to the other side of these visible material factors, i.e., the side of the invisible factors: the «**food chi**» in our daily bowl of rice. In nourishing and developing our physical visible body, we can rely on the adequate research studies in nutrition of the West. But for the nourishing of the invisible elements, i.e., the chi, within the body, just like the way the Royal Physician prepared the Royal Meal, we need to go back to the East in order to learn and understand the food chi. The ideal nutritional method would be a combination of both Western and Eastern ways.

Each food always includes two parts: the visible part (yin) and the invisible part (yang).

The material visible part, i.e., the yin part of foods, created by the yin chi, is the focus of the experimental scientific research studies on foods of the whole world. This part has been studied fairly acurately and sufficiently and, thus, provides us with accurate information about each food, for example for the apple, how many calories per 100g, the quantity of water, vitamins, nutritional facts, and ability to fight against which disease...

---

[13] 1 calory (lowercase c) is the unit corresponding to the volume of heat needed to increase the water's temperature 1 degree.

The invisible part is the chi part. The chi has two sides: the yin side and the yang side,[14] is invisible but helps move the visble part (for example blood) to crreate and nourish our body. We only observe and feel the invisible part through the reaction of the food chi in our body by induction. When you read this book, please temporarily forget your knowledge of experimental science and focus on the invisible chi in foods by applying with me the people in the old days' method of observing and feeling the invisible chi, and after that perform some experiment on your body to check and verify the presence and activity of the invisible chi in your body.

In order to express the meaning of the Chi, the Chinese character for Chi 氣 includes two parts:

- *the part* 气 *is the image of steam going up and becoming invisible in the air.*
- *chữ mễ* 米 *is the image of a bunch of cereals.*

Therefore, it is the image showing the fact that if we burn cereals (i.e., foods) we will create the invisible Chi.

About 5,000 years ago, the wise men observed phenomena in the universe and discovered that there were chi phenomena going down from the sky to the earth, such as light, wind ... and there were also chi phenomena going up from the earth to the sky like steam. These two chi phenomena flowing up and down without interruption and created all the visible physical phenomena of the world. The wise men drew an unbroken bar ———— to symbolize the yang chi going down from the sky, and a broken bar —— —— to symbolize the yin chi going up from the earth.

The two yin and yang bars interacted without interruption in accordance with the law of yin-yang [15] and created all the phenomena that we could observe in the universe.

---

[14] The Chinese character Yang 陽 has two parts: in the upper part, on the left is the secondary root for the Mountain, on the right is the character for the Sun, meaning the Sun is already up from the horizon; in the lower part is the word for Object 物 with the image of sun rays going down. The Chinese character Yin 陰 also has two parts: in the upper part, on the left we have the word Mountain and on the left we have the word Kim 金 looking like the house roof, in the lower part we have the word Vân 雲 (cloud), meaning covered by cloud.

Next, the wise men observed the yin-yang chi and the phenomena within their own bodies and felt that man was the image of the great universe and concluded that man was the little universe.

And from these two yin and yang bars, the wise men have written the I Ching, which, without any word, expressed the life process of men in the great universe.

At the present, in order to understand the invisible part, i.e., the chi, of foods, we must apply the method used by people in the old days in understanding yin-yang, and that is **OBSERVE** and **FEEL**.

1. Feeling The Chi

In the body of each person there is a flow of chi moving together with blood in the veins and forming a pair of yin-yang: blood (yin) nourishing the cells of the body, chi (yang) being the motor for the blood circulaton. Therefor we have the saying: *Khí tới đâu, máu tới đó* (meaning: where chi can reach, blood will be able to reach). Chi and blood move up and down, in and out, without interruption until we die. Chi and blood are like the car that moves to nourish the body, chi being the motor, blood being the fuel. Without the chi blood no longer circulates, that is why when the chi gets out of the body (death), the blood is still there but stops moving since the motor (Chi) is no longer there.

▪ Feeling the chi through temperature

According to the yin-yang theory, the chi expresses itself through the temperature. Warm or hot is yang chi, fresh or cold is yin chi. For example: after we consume foods containing many yang chi (alcohol, cinnamon, pepper…), our body gets hot, i.e, we feel the yang chi. To get our body's tempertaure down, we need to drink a glass of cold lemonade or eat watermelon… then we can feel the fresh yin chi in our body.

▪ Feeling the chi through blood

In our body, chi and blood form a pair of yin-yang and that's why foods are to nourish both chi and blood, i.e., both the body and the chi. This pair is inseparable throughout our whole life and only is separated when our body dies.

When we are still alive, the pair chi-blood can help us see the invisible chi through the color of our skin. Ruddy skin face characterizes nice blood flow or high health, but an irregular bloody hot skin face is the symptom of chi blowing up, possibly dangerous (stroke, CVA…), for example: after drinking alcohol, or when the blood pressure going up too high in older persons.

Standing for a long period in the open air, under sunshine or in cold weather, we would feel the fluctuation of through the changing color of the skin: bright red skin meaning chi is blowing out, pale skin meaning because of the cold chi has withdrawn inward.

▪ Feeling the chi through flavors

The yin-yang chi of foods are expressed through the odours and the tastes that our nose and tongue can feel. There are five kinds of odours (fragrance, fustiness, burnt smnell, urine odour, stench), which are the results of the yang chi blowing up and felt by the nose. There are five kinds of tastes (sour, hot, salty, sugary, bitter), which are caused by the yin chi, and felt by the tongue.

- **Feeling through pains**

A person is always subject to body pains, which medical examinations and tests could not identify the causes. Although it is scientically causeless, these pains could be caused by: weakened chi (chứng hư), stucked chi (chứng thực); that's why sometimes they could be treated by massages, coin rubbing, heat-producing oil application, moxa application, acupuncture because these treatments would help the chi get back to circulation.

2. The Yin-Yang Chi in Foods

In nature, plants and animals obtain the yin-yang chi naturally and create foods for mankind. Each food contains the natural yin-yang chi. The eating and drinking of mankind are for the induction of these yin-yang chi. In accordance with the developmental environment, the food chi tends to induce more heat or warmth (yang foods) or more freshness or coldness (yin foods) available in nature. Between these two tendencies, the balanced foods occupy the majority in quantity.

In the natural state, each food possesses two poles of chi: the yin pole originated from the earth and oriented toward the fresh or cold temperature, and the yang pole originated from the sky and oriented toward the hot or warm temperature. The amplitude of distribution of temperature between the two poles is the standard to make distinction of the yin foods from the yang foods. For example, if the yang pole is greater than the yin pole the result is the yang food, and vice versa.

Now, let's apply the experimental method in the identification of the yin-yang chi in our own bodies in order to identify the presence and activity of the invisible chi in our bodies.

▪ Chi identification testing method

In order to easily feel the chi in foods, the testing method needs to be based on the following conditions:

• *Select foods having extremely high yang chi (alcohol, cinnamon, pepper...) or extremely high yin chi (cold water, watermelon...).*
• *Intake a quantity of foods enough for a person to be able to feel the chi.*

We can feel the yin-yang chi in foods thanks to their temperature and movement.

The food yang chi gives us the feelings of:

• *Its temperature: warm or hot,*
• *the movement direction: blowing up (sky) and exiting out of the skin.*

The food yin chi is felt in the opposite direction:

• *Its temperature: fresh or cold,*
• *its movement direction: blowing down (earth) and entering the body.*

▪ Feeling of yang chi

Foods used in the experiment: alcohol, hot spices like cinnamon, black pepper, red pepper, ginger...

After a glass of alcohol, and a hot bowl of phở containing a lot of black and red peppers, how do we feel?

We feel the high temperature of the yang chi through this symptom: our body is warm hotter, our face is reddened, chi-blood moving fast and increasing blood pressure.

We feel the yang chi blowing up to our head (sky) and exiting out of skin resulting in reddened face, dizziness, with skin becoming hot and sweating.

These above-mentioned feelings are signals of the impact of the foods, and it helps us realize that alcohol, cinnamon, ginger... are yang foods.

▪ Feeling the yin chi

Foods used in the experiment: lemonade, watermelon.

In the hot weather of summer, after running, exercising... with your body being hot and covered with sweat, with your mouth dried, you drink a glass of cold water or lemonade or eating a piece of watermelon, how do you feel?

The feeling is: the body being fresh, relaxed, the body temperature going down. That feeling is caused by the impact of the fresh and cold lemonade and watermelon.

If we continue to drink too much cold water or eat too much watermelon, the yin chi will become dominating and exercising much pressure on the internal organs, such as the stomach, and, thus, will cause dizziness, weaken the body, and possibly diarrhea. That is the phenomenon of having too much yin chi in the internal organs and weakening the yang chi. These above-mentioned feelings confirm that cold water, lemonade, watermelon are yin foods.

The scientific experiments are objective, and, thus, persuasive while the observational experiments by oriental medicine are subjective by feelings, and only become persuasive after you have already felt the temperature of the chi, and, if you continue to use your own body as a laboratory to regulate it and balance the food yin-yang chi then this book will be useful.

3

Identification of Food Chi

Our daily foods are originated from the three following living environments:

The living yang chi environment of the sky for wild birds.

The living yin chi environment of rivers, lakes, seas for shrimps, fish, sea foods, algae.

The living medium environment of the earth for mammals, reptiles, plants, fruit, cereals...

From these living environments the flora and fauna live, grow, reproduce and become different in terms of the intensity of the yin-yang chi in accordance with the Four Chi (extreme yang hot, extreme yang warm, extreme yin cold, extreme yin fresh) and Five Tastes (sugary, hot, salted, sour, bitter).

Next, we observe the yin-yang chi of foods through standards of distinction (relative) by looking at the appearance (color, shape, position of growth...), by the contents inside (containing more or less water, lipids, number of calories...). In addition, we have to pay attention to the changes of the original temperature of the yin-yang chi caused by the cooking, processing, and preserving methods (refrigerator).

The standards based on the above-mentioned yin-yang principle only give us a general idea to make distinction the yin-yang chi in plants and animals, and help us, first, to perform the experiment to determine the yin-yang chi in each plant, and, second, to analyze the conflicts among the authors in their distinctions of yin foods and yang foods.

1. The yin-yang chi in plants

■ **Standards of color, characteristic, shape…**

The temperatures of the yin-yang chi of plants originated from the earth or in the water are revealed through colors, characteristics, shapes in the following list.

Standards	*Yang*	*Yin*
External color	Red, orange, yellow (tomato, pepper, pineapple…)	Green, purple, white (eggplant, cabbage, lemon)
Characteristic	Dry, light (spices like cinnamon, black pepper)	Much water or lipids (cucumbers, peanuts, oily nuts)
Shape	Long, pointed (carrot, red pepper)	Round, big (all kinds of potatoes developed in yin earth)

■ **Standards of odours**

The lung controls the chi, the nose is the window of the lung. The odour rising up belongs to the yang chi and enters the nose, and from the nose to the lung. Thanks to that we are able to know the intensity of the yang chi in the fruit and it helps us to classify them in accordance to the chi. For example, the jackfruit, durian, mango, pineapple… are yin fruit when they are still green (not having odour yet), but when they are ripe they will become yang fruit because of their intense odour.

▪ Standards of oils

There are two kinds of oils (vaporized oil and lipids) that help us determine that a plant is yin or yang. Plants like clove, nutmeg, cinnamon… belong to the group of hot yang chi plants because they contain lots of vaporized oils and can be dissolved in water. On the contrary, nuts like peanuts, chesnuts… belong to the group of cold yin chi plants because they give out oils under form of lipids.

▪ Standards of calories and water

Calory is yang, water is yin. Based on the scientific analysis findings regarding the volume of calories (yang) and water (yin) in each kind of foods, we can make the following distinction:

- *Yang foods: Foods containing more calories, less water.*
- *Yin foods: Foods containing more water, less calories.*

For example: Analysis of 100 g of some of the following foods:

100 g	Calories	Water (g)
Yang Foods		
Chocolate	500	1
Beef	165	70
Mutton	225	60
Yin Foods		
Cucumber	13	95
Watermelon	30	90
Lettuce	21	94
Equal yin-yang		
Apple	64	83
Grape	74	79

▪ Standards of minerals

Our body needs several principal minerals (calcium, phosphorus, potassium, sulfur, chromium, magnesium) and about 12 minerals contained in vegetables.

According to the yin-yang rule, we have pairs of yin-yang minerals going hand in hand. For example: the pair magnesium (yin) /calcium (yang), the pair potassium (yin) / sodium (yang). Potassium is yin because it lies inside the cells available in great number in vegetables and fruit, and its impact is to freshen the body. On the contrary, sodium is yang, lying outside the cells, making the chi blowing up and increasing blood pressure.

2. The yin-yang chi in animals

In the three living environments (sky, earth, water) there are living creatures. The temperatures of the food yin-yang chi are based on the two following factors:

- *Color of meat: red is yang, white is yin,*
- *Characteristic: Meat is yang vs fat is yin.*

1) In the sky (yang)

The very yang characteristic of foods from birds is expressed through the color red of their meat: for example, doves, sparrows, quails…

2) On earth: cow, sheep, chickens, ducks …

The intensity of the yin-yang chi is revealed through the color of the meat:

- *dark red indicating high level of yang chi temperature, for example: beef, mutton, goat meat;*
- *light gray and white indicating an equalized level of the yin-yang chi of the meat, for example: chicken meat, which rarely causes chaos in chi-blood.*

High consumption of red meat will cause diseases by too much yang chi (pimples, constipation) and high consumption of fat cause diseases by too much yin chi (obesity, high cholesterol).

3) In water (yin): shimp, fish, sea foods

The fish and shrimps live in a yin living environment (water), and, thus, provide yin low temperature to our body. Therefore, in order to achieve the yin-yang balance, people have to use the high temperature of some yang spices like ginger, red pepper to make the dip sauce when they eat raw fish salad, escargots, clams, oysters, cockles, shushi.

For sea foods, like cockles, clams, shrimps, crabs... they are divided into two categories according to their yin-yang temperture:

- *Category of yin low temperature: cockles, clams, oysters, excargots, squids;*
- *Category of yang high temperture: lobsters, tiger shrimps, sea crabs* (their yang chi revealed in the color red when well cooked).

5. Artificial processing

The foods that are artificially processed by industry, cooking, preserving (refrigerating, salting, drying, smoking...) belong to the group of foods of yin-yang unequaliziation. The food yin-yang chi have changed in accordance with the food preservation methods as follows:

- **Increasing the yang chi by steam** (yang) **and diminishing water** (yin)

Fresh foods that are fried, dried, smoked, salted will obtain more yang chi. Because of the loss of yin chi (water), this food will become highly yang, and, thus, can lead to diseases caused by yang chi like dried skin, pimples, high blood pressure.

- **Increasing the yin chi**

In Vietnam of the old days, the elders buried the wine in the earth (yin) to diminish the yang chi of the wine while the people in the West kept their wine in caves. Today, foods are preserved by cold air (refrigerators) or by freezing and, thus, artificially increase the yin chi of them; it will not cause any harm to healthy people but could be harmful to people having diseases caused by yin chi like diarrhea or cold skin.

4. Food chi can cause diseases

In nthe following list, we have selected a number of highly yang hot foods or highly yin cold foods, which, if we eat them excessively on a daily basis, could create chaos in our body's chi and cause chi-orignated diseases.

Foods	*Liquid spices*	*Vegetables*	*Fruit*	*Animal meat*
Hot yang chi	Cinnamon, cloves, ginger, back pepper, curry, anis, alcohol, beer, chocolate	Red ginseng	Durian, longan, lychee, jackfruit, pineapple	Beef, mutton, goat meat, goose, Thai duck
Cold yin chi	Cold water, chrysanthemum, lotus plumule, vervain leaf, tilleul	Bitter cucumber, cabbage, jicama	Sour grapefruit, lemon, lansium domesticum, passion fruit, star fruit, tamarind	Toad, snake, turtle, oyster, cockle, clam, escargot, abalone, jellyfish, sea cucumber, squids

4

The Chi of Flavors

After the Royal Physician had selected the ingredients for the prescription-meal, the đội Thượng Thiện (Royal Chef Team) used all flavors availble to prepare delicious dishes for the emperor.

For odours,[15] there are five of them (fragrance, fustiness, burnt smell, urine odour, stench) received by the nose, window of the lung, belonging to the **yang chi**, and, thus, blowing up to the sky and merged into the chi of the lung. Although generally speaking there are five odours, in the daily activities of the kitchen, people only pay attention to the fragrance.

For tastes, there are five tastes (sour, sugary, bitter, hot, and salty), which belong to the **yin chi**, and enter the body through the five internal organs (heart, liver, lung, kidney, spleen) The tastes are born from the yin chi of earth and are felt by the tasting of the tongue. According to ***Huangdi Neijing***, Chapter 9: Đất cung cấp ngũ vị cho con người… cây cỏ sản xuất ra ngũ vị (Translation: The earth provides the five tastes to mankind… plants produce the five tastes).

1. The Yang Chi of Odours

Thanks to the nose receiving the odours, we can feel the yang chi of plants. Under the heat provided by the kitchen fire or the sun

---

[15] Five odours: fustiness (liver), burnt smell (heart), fragrance (spleen-stomach), urine odour (lung), stench (kidney).

light, the fragrance, i.e., the yang chi, will blow up from the foods or radiate from the fruit or flowers. According to the intensity of the odours we will be able to know which plants or fruits contain more or less yang chi. For example, those fruit like pineapple, mango, durian, being highly yang fruit, will give much fragrance when they are ripe.

▪ Fragrance of fruit

The sesame seed contains a lot of yin chi under the form of sesame oil and when it is fried up its yang chi blows up and gives a very strong fragrance. That's why the brown rice (nourishing substances, vitamins, minerals), salt (yang), sesame (plentiful yin chi) can make the body healthy.

▪ Changes of chi from being green to being ripe

When the fruit is still green, the yin chi is dominant and, thus, it is sour. In its process of ripening, the acid yin substance (tannin, starch) becomes sugary, the yin chi (symbolizing the sour taste) partially transforms into yang chi (fragrance, color red or yellow), for example, pineapple, plum, orange, tangerine.

In some fruit, while still green, the dominant yin chi (tannin, starch) gradually changes to equalized yin chi (fragrant, sugary), for example, persimmon, banana.

▪ The chi between fruit and cover, leaf

The lemon contains very cold yin chi, while its leaf contains dominant yang chi that can be felt through the fragrance of the oil in it. The Vietnamese people cut the lemon leaves into small pieces to eat with the cooked chicken meat, or to season the field chicken (other name for rice field rat) before roasting. They also use lemon leaves in the vapour bath to treat cold and flu.

The skin of grapefruit or kumquat… contains dominant yang essential oil, and, thus, Vietnamese women put grapefruit skin in warm water to wash and clean their hair, making it shiny. The skin of kumquat mixed with honey can treat coughing effectively.

▪ Fragrance of ripe fruit

The ripe fruit that are sweet-scented are grouped into the category of fruit having extreme yang chi, such as durian, jackfruit, pineapple, longan… The people, especially those having dominantly yang internal organs, can only feel the yang chi if they eat too much (or daily) these kinds of fruit and when the dominant yang chi blow up and cause diseases such as lip impetigo, pimples, bleeding in bowel movement, or constipation. For example, during the season of longan ripening, everyone, who visits the longan farms in Bạc Liêu Province of the Chinese-Vietnamese from Chaozhou and invited by the owners to eat these longans free, knows that, after having eaten a lot of these longans they are offered a glass of limpid water from the container to "giải hỏa = eliminating the heat" caused by the longans.

▪ Fragrance of spices

The spices and aromatic plants, which have the fragrance blowing up, with the essential oil evaporating or dissolved in water, are grouped into the category of plants containing hot dominant yang chi, for example, cinnamon, ginger, clove, anis, nutmeg, which can be used in disease treatment. In addition, many aromatic plants like dills, mint leaves, basil, basilic, tarragon… also contain a little bit essential oil.

▪ Fragrance in religions

Almost all religions and folk beliefs use the fragrance blowing up to the sky from the burning of the incense or of the sandalwood or agarwood in their prayers, and in their approaches to the invisible world. In accordance with their ancestors worshipping, the Vietnamese people believe that smokes from the sandalwood incense, and the streaming hot worshipped meal will blow up into the invisible world so that the souls of the dead would be able to feel the respect of their descendants. For us, in our daily meal, we like to enjoy the fragrance of vegetables and fruits we eat.

Regarding medical treatment, odours are yang chi and enter directly into the lung because the lung controls the chi.[16] Therefore, in modern or traditional medicine, one of the treating methods is inhalation through the nose of some drugs under the oily form, such as menthol (for cough), and usually, for the Vietnamese people, when feeling like nausea, they inhale balm (Tiger balm).

▪ Treatment by odours

Odours are of **yang** chi, and, thus, blowing up, merged into the air of the sky, entering the lung because the lung controls the chi and the nose is the window of the lung connecting the lung with the outside. Therefore, odours are used to treat lung diseases and diseases of the internal organs caused by yin chi, for example, menthol vapour bath to treat COVID-19, could, cough, flu…

The Vietnamese people often use the very hot yang chi of odours to treat diseases caused by the cold. For example, they use ginger to treat the following diseases.

Ginger, containing from 1% to 3% essential oil in its cells, and radiating the fragrance, is used to treat and balance the yin-yang chi in foods. Regarding the disease treatment:

• *fried ginger mixed in boiled water or porridge is good to treat diarrhea.*
• *the North Vietnamese people often use ground ginger mixed with human hair in gua sha to treat cold and flu.*

---

[16] Heart controls blood, kidney does bones, stomach does meat, liver does tendon.

- people also suck a piece of ginger or ginger candy when feeling nausea caused by motion or seasick, airsick.
- in cooking, ginger is used to increase food digestion, especially to balance the yin chi when eating yin animal meat, such as cooked duck meat, or steamed oyster, clams, cockle, escargot...

2. The Yin chi in the Five Tastes

For all of us, the tongue is the organ giving us the five tastes (bitter, sugary, hot, salty, and sour). According to the Law of Wuxing (Law of the Five Elements = Ngũ Hành), the Five Tastes are closely related to the five internal organs of man:

- The bitter taste goes to heart.
- The sugary taste to spleen.
- The hot taste to lung.
- The sour taste to liver.
- The salty taste to kidney.

In order to clearly determine their relationships, let's perform the following experiment right on our body.

▪ Feeling the chi of the five tastes

Lung "hot"

The hot taste goes back to the lung. The lung controls the chi and the skin.

Testing. After consuming hot substances (alcohol, red pepper, black pepper...), the lung chi circulates fast leading to hot skin and sweating.

Application. Having observed that the hot chi of the hot taste (red pepper, alcohol, black pepper) activates the lung chi to circulate fast, the Vietnamese people, affected by a cold, often eat hot food (hot porridge containing a lot of black or red pepper…) after applying qua sha or taking a "vapor bath"[17] in order to have their body sweat. Sweating would expel the bad chi out of the body and help cure some diseases relating to lung chi such as cold or flu.

Kidney "salty"

The salty taste goes into the kidney and helps the kidney obtain the balance between the proportion of water with the salty substance obtained. The surplus salty substance will be discharged through urine and sweat. A quarter of the salty substances provided to our body was supplied naturally by our foods. The concentration of salty substances is high in meat, fish, sea foods and low in vegetables. The remaining salty substances are from the cooking, or by adding salt when eating, or from the additives during the industrial food processing and manufacturing.

Testing. The insufficiency of salty substances (sodium) will weaken the body, causing fainting, for example sweating too much after exercising or running. A glass of water mixed with salted lemon juice or of salted coke will help the body going back to normal because the salted substances will re-establish the balance between the level of water and salty substances in blood.

Application. In hot summer, when sweating a lot, the Vietnamese people often drink water mixed with salted lemon juice, or eat watermelon with a bit of salt.

Liver "sour"

The sour taste goes back to the liver. The liver controls muscle, tendon, finger and toe nails.

Testing. If the liver cannot function properly in balancing the chi-blood then it could cause diseases such as loss of appetite, indigestion, or heartburn, cracked or broken finger or toe nails…

---

[17] How to do the vapor bath: sitting in front of a pot of boiling water and covering one's whole body with a blanket.

Before the meal, eating some sour fruit (grapefruit, apple, plum, tangerine) or eating a dish of vinegared-salad would help with the heartburn since the sour taste forces the liver to discharge the bad substance and aid the stomach in its work.

Application. Having observed that the sour taste increases urination and decreases fat, some weight loss methods recommend the use of the sour substances (sour grapefruit, lemon, grapefruit juice, vinegar) to dissolve fat and increase urination. The danger of these methods is abusing the sour taste too much, which could lead to the weakening of the tendon of the bladder, causing increased urination and possibly hernia.

Heart "bitter"

There is bitter taste that excites the heart and also, bitter taste that calms the nerves.

The bitter taste that excites the heart. The bitter taste of coffee, tea, cocoa … is good for the heart chi and helps the blood circulation because the heart controls the blood and veins. The Westerners like the bitter taste of the caffeine of coffee and cocoa while the Oriental people prefer the bitter taste of tea.

Testing right on your own body by drinking one or two cups of very dense coffee or tea, and how do you feel? You feel your heart beating harder, and you are totally awake. That is the phenomenon of the bitter taste going into the heart and improve the heart chi.

Let's observe this scene on a rice field in Vietnam. Under the scorching sun, and sweating profusely, and yet, after having stopped his ploughing a short moment, the Vietnamese farmer drinks a bowl of fresh tea, smokes a cigarette, and he is back to normal, no more sweating. Why? It is caused by the bitter taste of the tea and the cigarette, which reinforces the heart chi.

Why does tea cause sleep loss and increase urination? Because of an abuse of the bitter taste, the heart has to work harder than normal, causing a chaos in the position of the heart and leading to sleep loss. In addition, the bitter taste increases the blood volume and blood pressure in the veins, causing an unbalance within the heart and the kidney (thủy hỏa bất tương giao = water and fire do not interface). In order to re-establish the balance, the kidney has to discharge more water in the veins, leading to an increase of urination. The Vietnamese people used to joke (nói lái = talking by inversing words) trà ngon, đậm đặc là trà «*thái đức*» (the two words "thái đức" are inversion of the two words "thức đái" meaning "being awake and urinate").

The bitter taste that calms the nerves.

In our body, there are two sources of fire (hỏa): 1) Quân hỏa (King fire) originated from the heart; and 2) Tướng hỏa (General fire) from the liver. These two fire chi flows usually cause the chi to blow up to the head, causing sleep loss, headache, hot-temperedness ... that's why the Vietnamese people often try to lower this level of fire chi by the bitter chi of animals and plants.

The bitter chi of animals: Snake bile porridge

The bitter chi of plants: Land bitter greens and sea bitter greens:

Rau đắng nấu cá trê vàng
(Bitter greens cooked with yellow catfish,)
Ngọt ngon vì bởi tay nàng nấu canh
(The soup is sugary and delicious because it is cooked by you.)

Bitter cucumbers.
«*Khổ qua kho cá rô đồng,*
(Bitter cucumbers cooked with field anabas,)
Miệng đắng nhưng lại ngọt lòng hương quê» - *(Ca dao)*
(The mouth feels bitter but the heart feels sugary and the fragrance of the fatherland.)- (Folk poetry)

Khổ qua mắc nắng, khổ qua đắng, khổ qua đèo,
(Affected by sunlight, bitter cucumbers become more bitter and too small,)
Dầu sanh, dầu tử, dầu nghèo em cũng thương
(In life, in death, in poverty, I always love you.)

Spleen "Sugary"

The sugary taste (sugar, cake, candy, pop, ice cream) goes directly to the spleen. The spleen chi controls muscles and brain activities. The sugary taste provides about 60% of the calories needed daily. When do we feel the sugary taste enters the spleen chi? It is when:

• Tired after hours of studying, thinking, book reading, because the innate chi (Ŷ = Idea) of the spleen has not received enough supply.
• Feeling the disintegration of the muscles, inability of concentration of ideas: symptoms of weakening of the spleen chi; the spleen controls the muscles and is the location of idea (Ŷ).

Some cakes, a glass of ice cream, or a cup of milk coffee will get the brain back to enthusiastic work, and that is because the sugary taste has reinforced the spleen chi and excites the innate chi (Ŷ = Idea) within the spleen.

▪ Principles of chi reinforcement

Although they are helpful to the corresponding internal organs, the tastes can still be harmful and cause diseases if they are abused.

Using the taste chi to reinforce an internal organ means that only an adequate volume is used to excite and balance the chi of that internal organ. For example, using a just adequate volume of the sugary taste will be enough to reinforce the chi of the spleen. We have to listen to the voice of our body with our feeling of "crave" or "enough."[18] For example, when we crave for something sugary then just eat something sugary because that is the signal that the spleen is weakened; when the craving stops then we stop eating anything sugary; if not, we will abuse the sugary taste and with the time, the voice of the body will no longer truthful, and will become the signal of disease like obese people always crave for sugary foods.

Any taste that is supplied too much and on a daily basis will cause harm to the corresponding internal organ. How do you feel

---
[18] This voice originates from the hypothalamus in the brain.

after you drink too much coffee or tea? The bitter caffeine causes harder heart-beating, nervousness, sleep loss, anxiety, wet hands. This happens because that high volume of bitter taste has excited the innate chi of the heart. Such daily abuse continues day in day out of the bitter taste could cause heart diseases. The spleen chi controls the muscles, and, thus, the result of the abuse of the sugary taste would be: obesity, a feeling of a heavy body, muscle, etc. This happens frequently with the Westerners.

In cases of heart diseases, high blood pressure, osteoporosis (kidney chi controls the bones), eating too salted foods on a daily basis would make the water chi (kidney chi) become dominant, overwhelming the fire chi (heart), causing some chaos in the heart chi. This phenomenon of no interface between water (kidney) and fire (heart), and the disease will get worse, and, that is why medicine always recommends less use or no use of salt.

In summary, although being helpful to the corresponding internal organs, the tastes could also cause disease if we abuse in using them. For example, the daily abuse of the sugary taste would cause: obesity, feeling of a heavy body, muscle pains. That happens very often with the Westerners, who do not know how to limit their consumption of sugary foods.

Part 2
Practical Use of Culinary Culture

For folk people, the practical use of culinary culture is using the invisible yin-yang chi in disease prevention, and, sometimes, in the treatment of diseases caused by the loss of balance of the food chi. After we have understood clearly the yin-yang chi in Part 1 and also have known about our own potential chi (hot or cold), we can learn from the experience of oriental physician Xuân Tàm in the application of food chi in disease prevention and in treatment of some diseases caused by chi.

We would also like to remind that food chi should be used only for ordinary, mild, and not life-threatening diseases caused by chi.

5

Potential Chi

Mai sớm một tuần trà,
(A round of tea in the early morning,)
Canh khuya dăm chén rượu
(Some bowls of alcohol at midnight)
Mỗi nhật cứ như thử,
(Have them like this every day,)
Lương y bất đáo gia.
(No physician will come to our home.)

In conversation, sometimes, I hear from Mr. A that I have hot chi in my potential chi, and, therefore I have to avoid hot foods, while Mrs. B has to avoid cold foods because she has cold chi in her potential chi. This is the way to describe the potential chi, i.e., temperature (hot or cold). Heat (hot) and coldness (cold) are the natural chi in the universe, but according to the law of yin-yang, when heat increases to its maximum could turn into fire, causing extraordinary phenomena. For example, during a period of drought, the heat turning into fire and could cause forest fires. In human body, people with hot potential chi, if consume too much hot foods, could make their internal heat turn into fire, causing extraordinary phenomena like pimples, constipation, nose bleeding … just like forest fires. These extraordinary phenomena are studied through the extreme yang chi and extreme yin chi in people's potential chi. People having these two chi states are often prone to chi-related diseases if they consume too much foods, of which chi are not compatible with their potential chi.

The third state of potential chi is the equalized chi state (relative balance between yin chi and yang chi) will not be mentioned here since it rarely lead to chi-related diseases caused by foods.

1. Very heat extreme yang potential chi state

Heat comes from the regular hot chi of the universe, but too much heat, like in the hot summer, can transform into fire that burns grass and plants (yin), just like the fire liver chi blowing up and burning its water (yin).

The inborn extreme yang chi state is revealed through 2 states of the chi:

- *State of normal health: body feeling warm, no symptom of chi blowing up and showing on the skin;*
- *State of heat transforming into fire: extreme yang foods, sunlight easily transforming normal heat into fire, causing yin chi-related diseases.*

The extreme yang chi state is revealed by the signal of the yang chi exposed to the outside like the skin becoming reddened and hot, causing the misunderstanding that the person is sick of yang chi-related disease. In reality, the yin chi is weakened by the too hot dominant yang chi, leading to symptoms such as constipation, nose bleeding, hemorrhoids. This is the phenomenon called «*Dương quá thịnh khiến âm bịnh*[19] = *Yang too dominant causing yin disease.*»

▪ Observing portrait of people with hot extreme yang chi state

The portrait of people with hot extreme yang chi state appears clearly after they have consumed too much hot yang foods (alcohol,

---
[19] Huangdi Neijing, Tố Vấn, Chapter. 5

hot spices...), causing the heat to easily and rapidly transform into fire. This phenomenon is easily identified through the following signals:
- *Skin becoming hot and reddened together with the yin substance (sweat) being expelled to the outside.*
- *Inside there are symptomps of yin chi level being lowered, such as constipation, thirsty.*

From these two main signals we are able to know which potential chi is burned by the hot yang chi (fire), for example:

- *Lung: skin is hot, pink or red, heavy breathing, head and chest covered with sweat, feeling easy with cold weather;*
- *Heart: head of tongue and face being clearly reddened* (except for the case of lower heat caused by weak yin), *feeling irritable, uneasy, and nervous;*
- *Spleen: traces of blowing fire appear on lips, red and swollen tongue with yellow surface, bad breath, and red swollen gums;*
- *Large Intestine: dried causing constipation;*
- *Bladder: being heated, less, darkened, and smelly urine, feeling hot and painful during urination;*
- *Body fluids being burned by hot chi, causing dried skin, lips and tongue thinned and dry, feeling thirsty and like to drink something cold;*
- *Extreme yang fire chi getting into the blood, causing nose bleeding, hemorrhoids, red pimples with pus, feces containing blood.*

▪ Feeling the signals of yin chi-related diseases

What symptoms occur when too dominant yang chi transforming into fire? Weakening and yin chi-related diseases.

Body weakening occurs because of yang chi blowing up, exiting out of the body, for example, a person, who drinks too much alcohol, will have his body reddened (chi exiting), and tiredness.

The too dominant yang chi will dry up the yin chi, causing diseases with the following signals:

• *Yin chi expelled to the outside: sweating, bleeding* (hemorrhoids, nose bleeding),
• *Yin chi dried up: body fluids dried up, causing thirst, constipation, uneasiness, too little urination.*

▪ The culprit

These above-mentioned symptoms are the victims of foods having too much hot extreme yang chi that cause harm to the yin chi. There are two kinds of these foods : foods of multi-chi and of poor nutritional value, and foods rich of yang chi and of nutrutional value as well.

1. Foods of multi-chi and of poor nutritional value. They are:

• *Beverages such as alcohol, beer,*
• *Ripe fruit such as durian, jackfruit, longan, pineapple, mango,*
• *Hot spices such as cinnamon, curry powder, ginger, black pepper, clove, anise, mustard …*

Eating **too much** of these above-mentioned foods and **on a daily** basis will result in a total loss of yin-yang balance (up-down, inside-outside) with the yang chi becoming too dominant and blowing up, causing symptoms such as headache, difficulty or even loss of sleep, uneasiness, nervousness, and painful urination.

2. Foods rich of yang chi and of nutritional value

The extreme yang chi of those foods like beef, mutton, goat meat, wild animal meat have impact on the blood. Those diseases like arthritis, skin diseases, reddened pus-covered impetigo, which cannot be treated with antibiotics, cortisone or antifungal drugs … are all results of extreme yang chi. The symptoms of infection, inflammation (impetigo, painful urination…) could be caused by two reasons: microbes or extreme yang chi.

First, one should consult a physician, and use antibiotics.[20] If after a few days the hot chi-related symtomps are not diminished (meaning not caused by microbes) then one must stop eating those above-mentioned foods having too much extreme yang chi and replaced them with yin foods.

- **Warning for men**

Regarding the health improvement, many Vietnamese people like to listen to sincere advices from friends, family members or newspaper articles, of which authors do not have knowledge of yin-yang chi. For example, for a friend who is sick or suffers of general debility, these people will automatically give advices such as: drink ginseng, or cinnamon powder mixed with honey, or even Emperor Minh Mạng's prescription so that «ông uống, bà sướng»[21] (meaning = the gentleman drinks, the lady is happy), or some beverage with hot pepper, clove, etc. These plants contain a lot of hot extreme yang chi, very good for people having low level of yang chi, but very harmful for people with extreme yang chi, probably causing chi-related diseases or worsening existing diseases. Therefore, before taking these sincere advices, you must know about your own potential chi states and the symptoms of having dominant or weak yang chi.

---

[20] A majority of medical doctors do not have knowledge of chi, and automatically apply this equation: Infection= microbes, microbes = antibiotics. If the sick person is not infected by microbes, the use of antibiotics is useless, but can cause harm to the intestinal bacteria ...
[21] Emperor Minh Mạng's prescription. A number of Vietnamese people pass around this prescription with a subtitle: "nhất dạ lục giao sanh ngũ tử, meaning = one night, six intercourses, giving birth to five children." I do not know if the subtitle is original or not but there is one thing that I know for certain: the prescribed drugs (in the prescription (that I got from a friend) are all helpful for yang chi (all of them also mixed in alcohol), and, thus the person who drinks it will feel extremely good and excited. If a person, who is in good health condition and has extreme yang chi state, listens to friends and uses this prescription, he will end up with the condition of too dominant yang chi, and too weak yin chi, and will become sick.

2. Cold extreme yin chi state

In a person with extreme yin chi state, the signal of insufficient yang chi appears outside (blue, cold skin, weak voice) and in yang chi-related diseases inside (diarrhea, flatulence, fear of cold ...). Âm thịnh thì dương bịnh[22] (meaning = Dominant yin chi causes yang chi-related disease) like the following portrait:

▪ Observation of portrait of cold extreme yin chi state

The cold extreme yin chi state is often seen in the following cases:
- *The people born with cold chi state,*
- *Serious diseases, old age, after surgery, excess of sexual activity, giving birth to too many children*

The main reason is that the extreme yin chi overwhelms the yang chi, causing weakening of the yang chi and leading to internal coldness. The symptoms of the weakening of the yang chi appear outside on the skin, and inside in the potential.

Because the yang chi is weakened, the symptoms are: short of breath, preferring hot drinks and foods, blue-gray skin, often feeling cold, muscle cramps, cold hands and feet, lack of enthusiasm, depressed, weak voice, loss of appetite, frequent urination and bowel movement, being sleepy all day long.

Because the yang chi of the spleen is weakened, the skin is cold, whitened, hands and feet are cold and weak, the sick person becomes obese, his veins are swollen, his belly is softened and swollen, he suffers from diarrhea, his tongue is wet and whitened, and he falls into sleep easily and all day long.

In addition, the yang chi of the kidney is also overwhelmed by the yin chi, causing too much urination, a signal of frigidity or weakened sexual activity (if the person is still young), constant fear, pale face skin, weakened back around the waist.

---

[22] **Huangdi Neijing, Tố Vấn, chapter 5.**

Anyone having this chi state should immediately avoid those extreme yin chi foods in order not to have his disease worsened.

▪ Recognition of foods having cold extreme yin chi

Extreme yin chi foods that are most often encountered are:

1. Animals: duck, frog, snake, clam, squid, raw fish (fish salad, shusi)…
2. Plants:
• *Greens and vegtables: bitter cucumber, spinach, jute vegetable, cucumber, cabbage, potato, turnip, sea weed …*
• *Fruit: lemn, passion fruit, grapefruit (sour), watermelon …*
• *Tea: chrysanthemum, lotus nut, vervain, tilleul, passion Flower, camomille…*
• *Cold water*

We'd like to remind that chrysanthemum is too much cold yin chi related, and is used in oriental medicine to treat high blood pressure, causing the body to be fresh and easily to fall to sleep. The Vietnamese people in normal health condition should be cautious, not abusing the royal chrysanthemum tea (chrysanthemum flower + one salted plum + one piece of rock sugar + 5 slices of licorice) for sleep.

▪ Warning for women

After good helpful chi is water, which is absolutely necessary for life. We can go several days without eating but we can't without drinking water. Water is absolutely necessary for the body (75% is water), cells (60% is water), and blood (95% is water)… From these observations, Western medicine often recommends drinking a lot of water (2 to 3 liters of water per day) and advises that the lack of water is the cause of dry skin, constipation although people still drink much water. That advice is applied to all people, regardless of the fact that women often belong to the group of people having dominant yin chi, and that abusing the cold yin chi of water could weaken their bodies (too much urination, frigidity, fear of coldness…), weaken their spleen chi (hands and feet becoming heavy swollen with water…), weaken their yang chi because their bodies must use a lot of heat to get the body water to 36º C …

In the West, we often hear the recommendation that we should drink a lot of water because water occupies 75% of the body, 60% of cells, and 92% of blood … Nobody can deny the absolutely important role of water, after the good and helpful chi, in all activities of the body. We must drink a lot of water when taking the medication prescribed by our doctors, when sweating profusely after exercising, and on hot days. Drinking water is absolutely necessary but it would be very absurd if we try to drink a lot of water when our body already has an excess of water or is having yin chi-related diseases (oedema, urination every 15 minutes causing sleep loss, bloating, frigidity…).

On the contrary, oriental medicine as well as nutritional technique both recommend that we should just drink enough water, and that drinking too much water could cause yin chi-related diseases. Why?

1. The chi of water is cold. If he drinks too much water, a person with extreme yin chi state will lose a lot of yang chi to heat his body water to 37º C, causing a more serious loss of yang chi.[23]

2. Diseases (stomach diseases, bloating…) caused by water or by the stomach chi becoming cold caused by eating too much cold foods or drinking too much cold water. That's why Chinese restaurants often serve hot teas during our meals. Stomach: drinking too much cold water while eating would lower the temperature of the hot yang chi of the stomach, causing bloating, heartburn[24] diarrhea, indigestion.

3. Drinking something hot. If not, the best way is, at thirst, drinking water just enough for the elimination of surplus substances from the body. The most dangerous way is eating too much cold

---

[23] Especially women (yin), who drink too much water (yin), will make yin chi dominant, causing harm to the yang chi, leading to too much urination, cold body ;
[24] It could be from the sweet dessert after the meal because the glucide stays in the stomach for only about 20 minutes before the fermentation begins, the blowing gas does not go down but goes down because it is blocked by the foods (meat, fish, cereals...) The best way to test is to stop eating sweet dessert after meal.

foods after giving birth when there is a lack of yang chi needed for cleaning the bad blood. That's why in the old days, women, who just gave birth, only ate and drank hot foods and beverages, lied on bed heated by burned coals mixed with salt and black pepper in order to tighten their belly skin just like during their young age, and also to avoid having tumor in their uterus.

4. Drinking just enough. In normal conditions, drinking water when feeling thirsty, just enough to eliminate the surplus substances (urea, uric acid, creatine, ammonia…).

5. Drinking too much water will increase the blood volume, and make the body work harder to eliminate the surplus water in blood in order to asist the heart. «*Drinking when not thirsty, eating when not hungry are the two things harmful for your heath.*» When do we know that our body needs water? Hypothalamus in your brain will send the needed signal for insufficience of water. When you are no longer thirsty you must stop drinking water, because if you do not listen to the voice of your body, hypothalamus will be in chaos and will give wrong signal. That's why many women, who drink too much water, are still thirsty, but their bodies will suffer from oedemas.

The role of the body is to regulate the volume of water in the body. Drinking too much water will cause harm to the kidney with the following symtomps:

- *The four limbs are cold, the back and knees are painful, the body lacks force, all caused by the cold chi of water becoming dominant and overwhelming the yang chi; the yang chi of the kidney is weakened, causing diseases like oedema, stomach disease.*
- *Lung* (upper organ) *and kidney* (lower organ) *are the two waterways that always connect each other* (proof: kidney moving up and down in accordance with respiration). *Therefore, if the lung is sick, it will weaken the kidney causing diseases in accordance with the law of mutual generation. For example, chronic asthma will cause harm to the kidney, leading to impotence, frigidity.*

In summary, the nutritional principle following the chi state is to achieve the balance between the yin chi and yang chi of foods by memorizing the two following basic things:

• *Yang foods are appropriate for the cold internal organ yin chi, and, vice versa, yin foods being good for hot internal organ yang chi,*
• *Eating too much yin foods will cause harm to the yang chi, eating too much yang foods will dry up yin chi;*
• *Therefore, on a daily basis, avoid to abuse only one kind of foods, either extreme yin or extreme yang.*

In case we have a yin-yang unbalance and become sick, at that point, we should apply the principle of food chi in treatment. For example, the internal cold yin chi causes stomachache, cold body, nausea, cold, diarrhea, menstruation pain… we can use hot spices such as ginger, black pepper, clove, nutmeg. In summary, maintaining the yin-yang balance by consuming the right extreme yin or extreme yang foods, we will be able to keep chi-related diseases away.

In the old days, the royal meal was a prescription, and today it is also a topic for our thinking on the pharmaceutical characteritics of foods for disease treatment and prevention, especially **diseases caused by chi**, and on having a life of good health by the practive of appropriate eating and drinking. Therefore, in case after a doctor's visit with the good results for all blood, urine, feces tests, but you still have these and those symptoms, then do not just think that «I have eaten good meals, I have listened to my doctor's advices, I exercise regularly…», and that's enough. On the contrary, you must think of:

• Eating and drinking not in accordance with your potential chi state, for example, you have hot chi state and still eating hot foods (alcohol, beer, mango, durian…) then your hot chi-related diseases will be worsened (hemorrhoids, pimples, high blood pressure…).
• Your have weakened kidney, too much urination, must wear diaper going to community meetings, and you still drink too much cold water instead of just sufficient hot water. From

this observation, in order to have a feeling about the chi of water you can do an experiment on your body (no difficulty, no cost) by drinking just enough water in accordance with your needs, and only drink hot water to see what happens.

With those readers who want to search and find the truth, they must know that each branch of medical sciences holds only one truth written in lowercase letters. The truth of medicine is efficiency, not great theories.

With those readers who do not believe in invisible things, for example «chi,» and believe only in what they can see, touch, and test, the author would like to ask them this question: in the United States of America, where we have the most advanced experimental sciences, and also where nobody has ever seen God, why everybody cherishes the US dollar bank-notes with large print letters IN GOD WE TRUST.

6

Uses of Food Chi

Besides the normal eating and drinking for personal survival, the people also taking advantage of the food chi for two objectives: *Increasing the chi forces and Balancing yin-yang chi.*

1. Methods of increasing the chi forces

In addition to the increasing of the chi forces by performing a number of nourishing exercises such as Sa Long Cương (name of a Vietnamese Kung Fu Club originated from Bình Định Province), Dịch Chân Kinh (Yi Jin Jing), Khí Công (QiGong), Tai Chi, Thiền Định (Yoga)... we also find ways to use foods to increase the chi forces in accordance with eastern or oriental methods.

▪ Western method

The western nutritional method is based heavily on the two following standards:

• *Harmony in body development: Eating and drinking aimed at achieving the balance between volumes of protein, lipid, glucide, vitamins, and minerals;*
• *Development of body force by obtaining a daily volume of calories needed for each person's activities.*

Why can calories increase the body force? In observing the sportsmen and the gym goers, we discover that *the more calories being burned the more chi they obtain*. Calories (heat quantities) are like the burned gasoline giving chi (chi) for the vehicle to move. Eating and drinking are the sources of supply of calories in order for the body to burn and transform into chi, which, in turn, will serve as the motor to move the body. The surplus calories will transform into fats serving as reserve chi to produce chi when needed.

▪ Oriental method

In the e-mail exchange between the older people, often there are advices to one another about the increasing of their body forces by using vegetables such as perilla leaves, ginger mixed with honey… and especially traditional medicinal wines. The advices are all very sincere, but because of lack of knowledge of food chi sometimes cause harm to their friends. For example, for people having hot potential chi (red and cracked tongue, headache, hemorrhoids, painful urination) who drink the famous Emperor Minh Mạng's medicinal wine called *"One night six intercourses"* would certainly have their diseases getting much worse. Therefore, before using foods to increase your chi, please do these things:

1) Review the lesson on Royal Meal (chapter 1) to understand that the increasing of chi means upgrading and maintaining the yin-yang balance in foods. For example, the sweet soup of longan eaten by the emperor had lotus nut (yin) stuffed in longan flesh (yang); duck meat (yin) dipped in gingered-fish sauce (yang).

2) Increasing chi means charging which chi being insufficient (either yin chi or yang chi) in order to re-establish the balance of chi. For example, after giving birth, or after serious illness, the body becoming pale, tired, feeling cold… signaling the insufficiency of yang chi. That's when people should consume yang foods such as ginseng, medicinal wine, hot water… to increase their body forces.

When we use foods to increase our body forces, we must know how to distinguish and feel: blowing-up chi and nourishing chi.

Blowing-up chi. When consuming too much a yang food, for example a medicinal wine,[25] and feeling some heat in the head or on the skin, that is the phenomenon of blowing-uo chi, which many people **misunderstand** as nourishing chi; this phenomenon is very dangerous, causing high blood pressure and tiredness afterward.

Nourishing chi. The nourishing chi exists only within the state of yin-yang balance. Therefore, after drinking alcohol (yang), one should drink a glass of no-sugar fresh lemon juice (yin) to balance the chi; when we fry some food, we should add a little bit of ginger (yang) to give some flavors to the food and make it easy to digest as well; yin foods such as sea foods, duck meat (yin) should be dipped in gingered fish sauce with red pepper (yang) to prevent diarrhea.

▪ Increasing yang chi

There are two types of plants that are extreme yang:

• *The type having fast and temporary impact: alcohol, pepper (both red and black) exciting yang chi (sexual activity) and chi on the skin (face reddened, sweating)*
• *The type having slow but lasting impact: ginseng, beverages from beans (red and black beans), maca, noni ...*

Ginseng symbolizes medicinal plants that are chi-nourishing, and very popular in Asia. There are types of ginseng in the market:

Red ginseng *(Panax ginseng) contains* a lot of nourishing yang chi, and, thus very helpful for people who are sick, old, or impotent. Who should not use red ginseng? Young and healthy people under 30 years old, people having high blood pressure (over 130/90), or chronic headache, nervousness or anger, or loss of sleep ...

---

[25] Alcohol is not a medicinal substance; it is only a solvent used as a medium for drugs, mostly used in the treatment of cold yin chi-related diseasesRượu không có tác dụng chữa bệnh mà chỉ là một dung môi để dẫn thuốc, phần nhiều dùng trong trường hợp điều trị một số chứng bệnh thuộc hàn chứng, or arthritis. Alcohol is not nourishing, and cannot make the body stronger like people used to believe.

White ginseng (*Panax quinquefolium*) and Siberian ginseng (*Panax quinquefolium*) contains less yang chi than Red ginseng, and, thus, is good for women, and people with high blood pressure.

Maca (*Lepidium mebenil*), ginseng of South American people, is grown a lot in the Andes highlands (altitude from 3500 to 4500 m), where it is very hot at day and very cold at night. Since the old days, the Incas considered maca as the sacred plant and used it to nourish their body chi. Peru produces a lot of maca in powder or pills. According to my personal experience, maca is equivalent to ginseng but at much lower price (especially if bought in Peru) and at the same time does not have too much taboos like ginseng, but if after drinking it one has difficulty in sleep then it should be avoided. There are too many legends about maca; in 2003, the football club Cianciolo won the South American championship, with a majority of players already over 30 years old, and their victory was explained that because they had drunk maca regularly.

Noni (*Morinda citrifolia*). 2000 years ago, on a number of islands of the Pacific Ocean, the Polynesians have used the noni fruit to make some kind of medication for upgrading their chi. Today, in the market, the noni fruit is sold in forms of fluids or pills. For the non-vegetarian people, they search and eat kidneys of pigs or oxen, goat meat, goat testicles, seal meat, etc.

▪ Inceasing yin chi of women: unguent, young antler…

The scratched, washed and cleaned antlers of deers and of tuttle shells are cooked to extract the essential substance and let it condensed into unguent, which is used to enhance yin chi. The young antlers of deers are also dried and ground into powder.

2. Balancing the food chi

After we have learned how to observe and feel the food chi, It's make a test of balancing the yin-yang chi. When there are symptomps of the yin-yang chi unbalance, we begin to feel by observing the signals of yin chi-related diseases or yang chi-related diseases.

▪ Yin chi-related diseaes

The too high consumption of yang foods (alcohol, cinnamon, durian, jackfruit...) makes the yang chi become too dominant and transform into fire burning the yin chi, causing constipation, nose bleeding, painful urination, bleeding hemorrhoids, dried body...

The way to get back the chi balance is using fire-lowering yin foods such as cold water, fruit, cucumbers, watermelons, chrysanthemum flowers... pure tapioca[26]

▪ Yang chi-related diseases

Abusing too cold yin foods like watermelon, cucumber, pennywort juice, cold water... could cause harm to the yang chi with symptoms such as diarrhea, feeling cold, thrill, too much urination... Foods giving much yang chi such as alcohol, dried rice grain, ginger, cinnamon... will re-establish the chi balance.

Following are some examples of using yin chi or yang chi of plants to balance the yin-yang chi for some ordinary diseases such as constipation, diarrhea, colds...

▪ Constipation

Constipation occurs because one eats too little fiber, or because the antibiotics create chaos in the living environment of the large intestines, such as a lack of lactic acid bacteria.

---

[26] Everyday drink one spoon of tapioca mixed in cold water, the hot feeling will be gone after two or three drinks. The tapioca bought in market usually is fake, mixed with other powders. You should buy it from merchants you know.

Observation

With healthy people, constipation is often caused by the food yang chi dries up the fluid in the intestines, causing these symptoms: feces becoming dry and hard and requiring a lot of forcing to get it out, cannot go for bowel movement when one wishes, cracked lips, thirsty, face reddened, bad breath, yellow and dry tongue. In this case, the natural treating method is using much cold yin chi foods to achieve a balance with the dominant yang chi.

Method of balancing the chi

After waking up in the early morning, squeeze two oranges into a glass of cold water, and drink the juice before eating breakfast in order to clean the intestines by the yin chi until having an easy bowel movement. Another way is drinking a lot of cold water, or eating much of yin chi foods such as cucumbers, watermelon, greens, sugar beet.

▪ Diarrhea

After having used antibioics without good results, and at the same time the feces test is also normal and determined not by bacteria, but the diarrhea still has not stoppe, the nit is time to think that the eating is not appropriate with the yin-yang chi law.

Observing then testing.

The very cold yin chi of foods often cause diseases of the digestive system, especially diarrhea with feces turning into sone kind of fuilds, with stomachache, loss of appetite, indigestion, loss of weight, and a weak body.

First, in order to know exactly if it is caused by the food yin chi, we must perform this following test:

- *Stop eating / drinking yin foods such as: cold water, raw or cold foods, and eat / drink only hot foods / beverages;*

- Apply compresses to the surrounding area of the navel with hot water for about 20 minutes.

If the diarrhea gradually diminishes, one feels easy, that's the signals confirming that the cold food yin chi has been the cause of the disease.

Principle of treatment.

Upgrading the yang chi by eating hot yang chi foods, and completely stopping yin chi foods is totally opposite to the treatment of constipation.

Using the yang chi of the following foods to neutralize the cold chi inside:

- *Hot beverages: 1. Ginger water: mixing deep-fried ginger sliceswith boiling water; 2. Carrot water: cooking carrots in water mixed with sugar and salt* (the sugary taste nourishing thr=e splen chi, and the salty taste nous=rising tyhe kidney chi);
- *Foods: using deep-fried rice to cook gingered-porridge; the hot food yang chi will re-establish the inside yin-yang balance; try to avoid alcohol, foods having too much fibers that could harm the intestinal membranes.*

When the yin-yang balance is already re-established, go bacl to the normal nutritional regime.

▪ Qua sha

Cold and sunstroke are the two nuances of wind-(or chi-) disease.

Cold is caused by a sudden weather change when the body is already weak, by getting wet in a rain, or by going out a night and catching the night dew… frequent symptoms are a runny nose, sneezing, mild headache and cough, fear of cold wind, preferingb to drink hot water.

Sunstroke is caused by the yang chi of sunlight invdsing the body after standing a long time under the sun. The symptom is a fever.

Most Vienamese refugees, who live in areas of cold climate and often catch a cold, should have to eat the following yang foods in order to expel the cold chi. The principle of treatment is using the hot chi to fight against the cold chi, nourishing the chi inside, and causing sweating so that the cold chi going out through the pores by the following methods:[27]

• *The method of vapour bath for sweating[28] and exciting the skin chi: sitting next to a large pot of boiling water containing essential oil with fragrant leaves, such as lemon grass, perilla, mint, ginger, bamboo..., with the whole body covered by a blanket, in oder to get sweating in order to expel the cold chi through the pores… Now, overseas, we can go to a spa for a steam bath for sweating, and then eat a large bowl of very hot vegetable soup or a bowl of above-mentioned porridge. This sweating method cannot be applied to people with a weak body, having dizziness, or old people, or people haing heart diseases* (because sweat is internal fluid of the heart).

• *After that, eat a bowl of very hot porridge containing hot spices* (black or red pepper, garlic, ginger. Using a similar method, the Jamaican people drink very hot black pepper tea to treat colds. ởi Jamaïque uống trà hạt tiêu (poivre de la Jamaïque) thiệt nóng chữa cảm lạnh.

▪ Treatment by fragrance

Cinnamon, clove give essential oil to drink or massage, heating the skin, fighting the yin diseases (slow digestion, late menstrual cycle, stomachache, nausea). Abusing the essential oil of cinnamon could caue diseases, therefore, European food industry makes a regulation to have only 2mg of the fragrant coumarin from cinnamon in 1kg of food. In Germany, the children (weighing under 15 kg) are recommended that they should not eat more than 4 cakes containing Zimtsterne cinnamon a day to avoid nose bleeding.

---

[27] In Vietnam therei another treatment called Qua Sha (cạo gió, especially to treat sunstroke) to treat colds, fighting the colds by using a chicken egg with a silver coin, or by fried bran, or by ground ginger mixed with alcohol.
[28] The cold chi will be going out together with the sweat.

Ginger contains from 1 to 3% essntial oil in its cells, giving out the fragrance, and is used to treat and balance the yin-yang chi in foods. In disease treatment, ginger is used very much, such as:

• *fried ginger slices mixed with boiling water or cooked in porridge to treat diarrhea,*
• *Vietnamese people in the North used ground ginger mixed with hair in qua sha to treat colds,*
• *keep in your mouth a piece of ginger slice or candy to prevent nausea when you travel and get seasick*
• *in cooking, using ginger to give some flavor to the foods and help the digestion, especially to balance the yin chi when eating yin foods, such as cooked duck meat, oyster, clam, escargot...*

▪ Iced or hot water?

Whoever does not have shoulder pain, back pain, knee pain? The commom advice is to apply ice bag and to take pain killers. Incase the pain becomes chronic and taking dru gis just like eating candy, then one has to think again and ask questions.

There are two types of pain: Inflammatory pain, and chi pain (or chi-related pain).

1) The four characteristics of inflammatory pain are: skin at position of the pain is reddened, swollen, hot and painful. In this case, the coldness of iced water will help to reduce or even possibly cure the pain because the cold yin chi (iced water) eliminates the hot yang chi (hot, red, swollen).

2) If it is only painful without any of the other symptoms like swelling, reddening, and hotm, then it is chi-related pain, and one has to use hot chi of water[29] or moxa[30] helping the bood circulation to stop the pain. If instead one applies ice bag the pain will become chronic. This is my personal exprience (Xuân Tàm, oriental medicine doctor),

[29] If using hot water, use a rubber hot water bottle bought at pharmacy.
[30] Moxa is the mugwort that acupuncturists use to heat.

who has treated many such cases, zand, thus, you should go ahead and perform the test, which is of no risk and no cost. This test is very necessary for old people suffering from **back pain** before making decision for risky and costly treatment.

«Old age is just following behind us»

When we were still young, our potential chis were still functioning well, we could eat what we like, and it was OK. But when we reach retirement age, with all kinds of diseases, it is about time for us to think about our past but also about what we should eat and drink for our health in the remaining years of our lives.

Finally, the author would like to remind the readerds, especially old people, that although advices given to you by friends and family members are very sinncere, you must know the following things:

- *Your potential chi are cold or hot;*
- *Identifying the chi of foods to know if they can be accepted by your body not not;*
- *After having consumed the foods, follow the abnormal reactions of the body. For example, after drinking of pennywort juice, you have stomachache and diarrhea, it means that the juice (yin) is not OK with your potential chi (yin), or drinking medicated wine makes your blood pressure going up then you must stop immediately.*

Part 3
CULINARY CULTURE IN SPIRITUAL LIFE

Today, the majority of the Vietnamese people still worship their ancestors at home and the deities at Community halls and temples. The characteristics of this ancestor wroshipping are:

• *organizing of the copious worshipped meals in front of the altars,*
• *praying and inviting the ancestors' or deities souls to come-back and enjoy the meals.*
• *after the meals being enjoyed by the ancestor or the deities, the ordinary dishes of the the worshipped meals become «divine = linh 靈».*

Why is there this belief in the culinary culture? In order to answer this question, we need to understand the three following things:

• The concepts of soul *(hồn)* and spirit *(vía or phách)*
• The meaning of sacred, divine *(linh thiêng)*
• Ordinary foods becoming «sacred, divine» *(linh)*

▪ Soul and Spirit

Soul (Hồn 魂) is the very sacred spiritual part of a person, and, thus, is called linh hồn (sacred soul); the sould resides in tâm 心, i.e., heart (Tâm hồn: 心魂). After death, the soul flies up to the sky.

Spirit (Vía) is the Vietnamese or synonym of the sino-Vietnamese **phách** 魄. Vía[31] is the dark side of soul, i.e. the yin chi of soul, and, thus, soul-spirit (hồn vía) often going hand in hand like a pair of yin-yang.[32]

During lifetime, the spirit resides in the lung, and it intertwines with the soul; at death, the soul and the spirit are separated.[33] After death, the **spirit** (vong hồn = dead soul) **still remains on earth**,[34] sometimes it appears and we often call it ma[35], quỉ[36]. Because of the belief that the spirit still remains on earth, and, thus, in our culture, we offer foods at homes and in community halls as worshipped meals to the spirits of the dead people.

▪ Sacred (Linh thiêng)

When talking about the invisible world, we often use the phrase «*linh thiêng*» (sacred) to talk about the dead souls of our ancestors, or of the deities.

▪ Linh 靈 (Divine).

The pure top chi of the yang chi is called thần 神, the pure top chi of the yin chi is called linh 靈. Therefore, the dead person is called

---

[31] According to Thiều Chửu's dictionary, Vía is the top spirit of the people. When the top spirit is exhausted, the physical remain is called phách

[32] Common saying : "*thất hồn lạc phách*" 失魂落魄 no more soul, no more spirit, or "*hồn phi phách tán*" 魂飛魄散 soul flying spirit dissolved. .

[33] In the poem-novel «*Đoạn trường tân thanh*» (i.e. Thúy Kiều's story) there is a sentence: «Kiều rằng những đấng tài hoa, Thác là thể phách còn là tinh anh» (Kiều said : «For the talented people, only the phách dies, the top spirit will remain.»)

[34] Innthe village of Nam Sơn, Bắc Ninh, the ancient pagoda Hàm Long helps followers «*nhốt vong*» (Incarcerating the dead souls) of people , who have been dead at « *giờ Trùng*» (Bad hours).

[35] Ma (Ghost) is the Chinese word translted from the Indian word Mảra, used for the God of Passion.

[36] Quỉ (Evil ghost): dead souls of ordinary people, little people; Thần (Deity) : dead souls of kings. Mandarins, noble people …

linh, meaning that although the physical substance has already been dissolved, the pure top chi of the yin chi still remains on earth and is called vía, or phách, and, thus, establishing the worshipping tablet is called thiết linh 設靈.

▪ Thiêng (Sacred)

The Vietnamese word Thiêng used together with Linh (Sino-Vietnamese) to designate something miraculous, or of revelation. From the invisible world, the souls of the dead person or of the deities «*hiển linh*» (self-reveal) and make the living people feel their presence, then that is called linh thiêng. The phenomenon of self-revelation like this is the foundation of the Vietnamese people's belief in the worshipping of ancestors, of deities, and the survival of the Mẫu Cult, of the medium sessions from the pre-historic era.

▪ Why does an ordinary food become sacred?

The good fortune granted by the deities as well as the foods enjoyed after the offering ceremony to ancestors are seen by the Vietnamese people as sacred with the positive support effect to the living people. In order to understand it, please pay attention to the following things.

Participting the greeting ceremony of «ông Bồ[37]» in the festival of Đồn Sơn, village of Yên Đức (Đông Triều Province). «Ông Bồ» is a pig, an ordinary domestic animal. Why is a pig respectfully called «Ông Bồ» by the people?

This common question of the Vietnamese people is answered by the people of Yên Đức village as follows: «When the pig (though people used to say : stupid like a pig, pig face…) is connected to the rites of the ceremony, and is enjoyed by the dead souls of the deities,

---

[37] Called "*ông Voi*" at the festival in the community hall Trà Cổ, Quảng Ninh Province, organized on the 1st day of the 6th month of lunar calendar every year.

it becomes sacred by the spiritual factors of the deity worshipping.» That is the reason that the meals offered to the ancestors, to the deities are considered as sacred. That is the intangible cultural factor of the culinary culture.

Greeting ceremony of «ông Bồ»

Greeting ceremony of "ông Voi" at the festival in the community hall Trà Cổ, Quảng Ninh Province, organized on the 1st day of the 6th month of lunar calendar every year

7

Worshipped Meal
Culinary cultural symbol of religions

According to the folk beliefs, after being placed on the worshipped meal trays offered to the dead souls of the ancestors or the deities, those ordinary foods have become **sacred.**

The following conditions are required to make the worshipped meals sacred:

- *Position.* The worshipped meal must be placed in front of the ancestors' or on the deities' altars where their dead souls reside.
Ambiance. In order to create a pure and fragrant ambiance, people burn incenses, or sandalwood to greet the dead souls coming back and enjoying the offered foods.
Dishes. The whole meal also must be hot, fragrant, and covered with incense smokes whirling up; the fragrance (odour is yang) of foods flying up for the souls (yang) high above can enjoy; the 5 tastes (sour, hot, sugary, bitter, salty) in the foods are reserved for the dead souls (yin) of the dead people and for the descendants to enjoy.
Respect. The worshipped foods should not be eaten in advance, the cooking also must be very careful, and considerate; the presentation must be solemn and respectful.

Remembrance. In addition to ordinary dishes used to offer in worshipping ceremonies for ancestors, there should be one dish the dead person liked when he was still alive. For the worshipped meals offered at community halls, there should be one more dish called «hèm» which was the preferred dish of the deity, for example, the «hèm» of the village of Đình Bảng is the rat meat dish.

For worshipped meals, we have:

The worshipped meal at home: offered to the dead souls of ancestors on their death anniversaries, and to the deities at Tết (the Kitchen God, the Hành Khiển Mandarin).
The worshipped meals at community halls,
The worshipped meal for ancestors at Tết.

1. Worshipped meal at home

▪ Worshipping ancestors on their death anniversaries

The tray of the worshipped meal is placed in front of the ancestors' altar in a very solemn atmosphere with incense smokes whirling up. The family head prostrates, prays, and invites the dead souls of the ancestors to comeback and enjoy the offered foods. Next the descendants take turn to come and prostrate in front of the altar.[38]

---

[38] The altar is the universe in miniature in accordance with Taoist philosophy, serving as residence for the dead souls, and, thus, the objects on it are arranged as follows: the round incense holder symbolizing "*Vô Cực*", and the bronze sandalwood burner symbolizing "Thái Cực" are placed at the center, with two candle holders on both sides symbolizing yin-yang; the whole set symbolizes Wuxing: Metal (Kim, bronze burner, candle holders), Water (Thủy, tea, alcohol), Wood (Mộc, incense sticks, chopsticks, frame of tablets, Fire (Hỏa, the lamp), Earth (Thổ, sands in the incense holder, the bolder in ceramics); Three Treasures philosophy (Sky-Earth-Man) is represented by the 3 bowls of water or alcohol or by the set of Tam Sơn.

Ancestors' altar *The worshipped meal*

The worshipped meal in the North.

The traditional worshipped meal of Vietnamese people in the North always includes dishes such as: steamed sticky rice (of green beans, peanuts, or spiny bitter gourd), boiled chicken meat, pork sausage, boiled pork, boiled chicken eggs, fried vermicelli with dried bamboo shoots, black mushrooms.

worshipped meal in the North

The worshipped meal in the South.

The worshipped meal should be decent and includes all four kinds of dishes: one stewed dish, one boiled dish, one fried dish, and one fish-sauce-cooked dish.

- Stewed dish: Pork stewed with bamboo shoots; bones stewed with vegetables ...

• Boiled dish: Boiled thin slices of bacon, boiled chicken meat ...
• Fried dish: Fried vegetables, fried daikon ...
• Fish-sauce-cooked dish: Fish-sauce-cooked pork, or snakehead with coconut juice ..

worshipped meal in the South

▪ Worshipped meals for family protector-deities

From time immemorial, at every spring comeback, our people prepared to enjoy Tết: making preparations for a copious meal, wrapping the square and cylindrical sticky rice cakes, cleaning the ancestral altar... and then putting up the Tết Pole as the signal for Tết greeting.

▪ Worshipped meal for the Kitchen God

On the day of putting up the Tết Pole, the 23rd day of the 12th month (lunar calendar), the Kitchen God would make his trip back to the Heaven, the family would prepare a worshipped meal to say good-bye to him. The meal must include a carp so that the Kitchen God could cross the Vũ Môn[39].

---

[39] The Kitchen God is the deity assigned to Earth by the Jade Emperor to protect families, and to record all good and bad things people do, and on the 23rd day of the 12th month he would comeback and report to the Jade Emperor. Why do we have to offer the carp? In order to fly up to the Heaven, the Kitchen God needs to ride the carp because when crossing the Vũ Môn (Rain Gate) the carp will become the dragon and will be able to continue the trip.

Worshipped meal offered to the Kitchen God, including a live carp

- ## Worshipped meal offered to Hành Khiển Mandarin at midnight before Tết

Every year, the Jade Emperor assigned to the Earth the Hành Khiển Mandarin (Đương niên chi thần = Mandarin of the current year) to govern the people in 12 months with the assistance of Hành Binh (a military officer) and Phán Quan (responsible for records). Every year, exactly at midnight before Tết, the handover of work between the old and new Hành Khiển mandarins, and that's why that night is call Trừ Tịch night (Trừ is giving back the position title, Tịch: the night, i.e., the night of the last day of the 12th month, when the current year ends, and the new year begins). The worshipping ceremony at the midnight before Tết is carried out in the open air, in order to greet the celestial guards of the Hành Khiển Mandarin because all the deities circulate between Earth and Sky during Tết, and, therefore, the Tết Pole, symbolizing the axe of the universe joining Sky and Earth, is playing the role of a ladder for the deities going up to the Heaven, and that's why the Tết Pole should have bamboo leaves attached to the top, looking like the clouds, and the people compte with one another to have their Tết Poles as high as possible.

Worshipped meal for Hành Khiển Mandarin at midnight before Tết

2. Tết worshipped meal

According to the tradition, on the 1st day of Tết, every family prepares a very copious meal for Tết, first to offer to the ancestors in accordance with the filial duty, and second, for all family members enjoy the meal, like the saying "Đói giỗ cha, no ba ngày Tết" (meaning: hungry you celebrate your father's death anniversary, getting full at the 3 days of Tết). All of the three North, Central, and South regions of Vietnam keep that common custom, but, in terms of the dishes for the worshipped meal, it could be different depending on their historical and economic conditions. North Vietnam, with the cultural centre Thăng Long, has a thousand-year long history of stylish and elegant culinary art, and, thus, its banquet or feast meal has been well known in our culinary culture, and, today, its traditional Tết meal still is the standard for the whole country, in terms of living manners, of elegance; it is like a culinary poem of Thăng Long handed down to new generations. On the contrary, the Tết meal in South Vietnam reflects right away the rich, relaxed, non-squeamish life of the new land.

▪ Tết copious meal in North Vietnam

Square sticky rice cake
Bên ngoài xanh lá dong xanh,
(Green dong leaves outside,)
Bên trong nếp đỗ mỡ hành hạt tiêu.
(Sticky rice, fat, onion, pepper inside.)
Gói nghĩa tình, gói yêu thương,
(Wrapped with gratitude, wrapped with love,)
Dẻo thơm từ thuở Lang Liêu tới giờ.
Soft and fragrant from the Lang Liêu time to the present.)

Many Northerners, of the middle class, or intellectuals, are fond of formality, and, thus, their Tết Meal is prepared very carefully, fastidiously, with all kinds of foods, nicely displayed, and arranged in accordance with the regulation of tứ trụ 四柱, i.e., every Tết copious meal[40] should have at least 4 bowls, and 4 plates to play the roles of 4 pillars supporting the copious meal.[41]

Tứ trụ with 4 chiết yêu bowls[42]:
1 bowl pig foot steamed with bamboo shoot,
1 bowl of vermicelli cooked with chicken organs,
1 bowl of swim bladder cooked with chân tẩy[43] and chicken broth,
1 bowl of ground pork and mushroom soup.

Tứ trụ with 4 plates of foods as follows:
1 plate of cooked chicken with tiny sliced lemon leaves, to be served with salt and pepper in lemon juice,
1 plate of cooked pork,
1 plate of Vietnamese pork sausage, fried sausage, head cheese, pig ear sausage,
1 plate of cinnamon pork sausage.

Tết Meal displayed in 4-pillar arrangement

---

[40] The summit of Hà Nội's culinary art is the cỗ (cm = copious meal): Cỗ tứ quí (four-treasure cm), cỗ cưới (wedding cm), cỗ nhà đám (funeral cm), cỗ một tầng (1-story cm), hai tầng (2-story cm), or cỗ ba tầng (3-story cm), bốn tầng (4-story cm); in the old days, there was a guild specializing in preparing cm for a price

[41] Today, many people do not understand the word trụ (meaning cột = pillar), and, thus, give wrong definitions for tứ trụ as four seasons or four directions. From the concept of tứ trụ, rich or noble people make arrangements of copious meals with 6 bowls, 6 plates or 8 bowls, 8 plates. The extra four bowls include one bowl of soup of well-cooked thread-like sliced German turnip, one bowl of steamed whole pigeon, one bowl of steamed chicken, or abalone or shark fins. The extra four plates include ne plate of frozen meat, one plate of head cheese, one plate of fried nem, one plate of salad made of German turnip, or of spinach, or rolled romaine lettuce with fermented glutinous rice. The copious meal is displayed in many levels, with a bronze tray in the middle, and, thus, people used to say «mâm cao cỗ đầy» (High tray, meal full). The fuller the tray the respect for the ancestors more profound, reflecting the skills, and preparations of the chef cook.

[42] Chiết yêu bowl: type of medium-size bowl, smaller from the middle toward the bottom.

[43] Chân tẩy includes: German turnip, carrot, beans all sliced in form of beautiful flowers.

The foods contained in *"tứ trụ"* bowls and plates are mostly concentrated in 4 words «giò nem ninh mọc» (sausage, nem, steamed food, ground meat). Giò (sausage), chả (steamed mix of scrambled egg with ground meat), nem (fermented mix of ground pork and shredded pig skin) hold the central place of the Tết copious meal. The main reason is that the Northerners pay much attention to the order of food eating: they enjoy the foods on the plates first, usually with some sticky rice eating and with some alcohol sipping. After that, they will enjoy the foods contained in the bowls.

In addition to the foods in the *"tứ trụ"* bows and plates, the other required foods include:

Bánh chưng (square sticky rice cake) accompanied by pickled onions,
A plate of spiny-bitter-gourd-flavored sticky rice so that its color (red) would bring good luck.

Soup of dried bamboo   Plate of fried Nem   Plate of Ground port sausage

Pickled Onions   Frozen meat   Spiny-bitter-gourd-flavored sticky rice

▪ Tết copious meal in Central Vietnam

Sour Nem

Lá chuối xanh êm một khoảnh vườn
(Green banana leaves from a part of the garden)
Giấu miếng đêm hồng khe khẽ hương
(Hiding the pink and slightly perfumed piece of meat)
Dâng chút lên Tiên từ da thịt
(We offer to the Fairy that piece of meat and skin)
Thoả thú bình dân lẫn Đế vương.
(That satisfies the taste of people and Kings.)

The basic foods often offered in the Tết copious meal in Central Vietnam include: **cooked chicken, pork, bánh tét** (cylindrical sticky rice cake), **sour nem**, pickled onion, **spring rolls** ... In addition, people from Central Vietnam also pay attention to the factor of preservation, and, thus, many of them often prepare salted foods, such as pork cooked with fish sauce, salted shrimp, fried chicken, nem, meat immersed in fish sauce ...

Specifically, people from Central Vietnam like very much to eat rolled foods, such as cooked pork, steamed fish rolled in rice paper, skewed nem ...

Black-peppered beef sausage

Sour nem

Pickled vegetables

Pork immersed in fish sauce

Molasses beef stew

Tổ cake (sticky rice, ginger, sesame)

▪ Tết copious meal in South Vietnam

Bánh tét (Cylindrical sticky rice cake)

Nếp xào thơm dẻo đậm đà,
(Sauted sticky rice really flagrant,)
Đậu bùi, chuối ngọt nhìn qua là thèm
(Soft beans, sweet banana, just a look gives appetite,).
Sợi mỡ béo ngậy hoà thêm,
(Rich thread-like slices of fat adding more taste,)
Thành hương vị bánh độc quyền Vĩnh Long.
(Producing the special flavor of the exclusive cake of Vĩnh Long.)

Contrary to the cold weather of North Vietnam, South Vietnam enters the Tết period within an atmosphere still having warm sunshine. As a region of abundance in local products with numerous kinds of fruit, South Vietnam offers an extremely rich Tết meal, which does not care much about formality, and regulations like in the North. In reality, the Southern Tết copious meal deeply reflects a rustic, unsophisticated culinary culture in terms of preparation and display, using a lot of ingredients taken directly from the nature, rather than from raising and growing.

The main foods include: pork cooked in fish sauce and coconut juice (some /over-cooked, some with duck eggs), served with fermented bean sprouts or pickled leeks, stuffed bitter cucumbers, pig ears immersed in sweetened vinegar, salad of lotus roots, Chinese sausages, head cheese, boned chicken, cooked pork dipped in fish sauce, spring rolls, salad of shrimps and lotus roots, pork offal, bamboo shoot soup (with fresh bamboo shoots, not dried ones like in the North)…

***Thịt kho** mềm bở mỡ loang*
(Fish-sauced pork soft and fatty,)
*Tô vàng **trứng** mỏng điệu đàng vây quanh*
(Nicely surrounded by thin slices of scrambled duck eggs)
*Ăn cùng **dưa giá, hẹ xanh***
(Served with **fermented bean sprouts**, and **green chives**)
Khổ qua dồn thịt, món canh mát lòng.
(**Bitter cucumber** stuffed with meat makes a refreshing soup.)
(Poem by Bạch Liên)

More special is the bánh tét (cylindrical sticky rice cake), always served with a plate of fish-sauce-immersed white radish.

Sắc hương ngày Tết thêm gần
(With all its colors and fragrances, Tết is approaching)
Đôi câu đối đỏ sáng dần mực xưa
(A couple of red-inked parallel sentences gradually shining)
Rộn ràng đợi phút giao thừa
(Emotionally waiting for the transition to new year)
Bánh chưng bánh tét cũng vừa ngát hương.
(Bánh chưng, bánh tét are displayed in their full fragrances.)

Tết copious meal in South Vietnam

Pickled pig ears   *Stuffed port in pig stomach*   *Bitter cucumber soup*   *Fish-sauce-cooked pork with eggs*

5. Worshipped meal at community hall

The belief in the fact that the dead soul of Thành Hoàng can enjoy the worshipped meal and protects the villagers is a characteristic of the intangible aspect of the community culinary culture. In the countryside, the official worshipped meal at the community hall is organized on the festival day to celebrate Thành Hoàng. The two principal activities related to the worshipped meal offered to Thành Hoàng are:

Competition of rice cooking.
Killing chicken, pig and cow.

▪ Cooking rice for the worshipped meal offered to Thành Hoàng

Many villages in North Vietnam still organize the competitions of rice cooking at the community hall's yard[44] both for worshipping of Thành Hoàng and for preserving the tradition of good rice cooking competition. The cooked rice will be offered to Thành Hoàng in the ceremony. After that, it will be offered to the invited village officials and elders. The custom of rice cooking competition is to **preserve the tradition of good rice cooking** in an agricultural country.

▪ Rice cooking competition at Thị Cấm village

Every year, on the 8th Day of the First Month of the lunar calendar, the people of the Thị Cấm village (Xuân Phương ward, Nam Từ Liêm district, Hà Nội) get together in the yard of the community hall to

---

[44] The competition of rice cooking is a game that has changed gradually... In some place, each person has a stove, a piece of young bamboo branch, and a knife; everyone has to whittle the bamboo branch and blows the stove, using the bamboo pieces to burn the stove. The one finished first with a pot of cooked rice wins the competition. At another place, the competitor has to chew sugar canes and uses the bagasse to burn the stove. The rice cooking competition of Chuông village, Hà Đông province, is very difficult. There are two different competitions. In the competition for girls, the competitors have to cook rice and at the same time babysit a child of another person and also keep a toad put in a circle. Who has cooked a good pot of rice and at the same time helped the child not crying and also kept the toad within the circle wins the competition. In the competition for boys, the competitors have to get the boat with all the needed objects across the pond. The stove is on the bank, and the competitor sits on the boat. In some village, the competitors have one hand holding a live duck, at the same time carry on his shoulder everything he needs, such as the pot, the stove, rice, water, wood, and cooks rice while walking. The Tích Sơn village, in Vĩnh Yên province, has the rice cooking competition organized at the beginning of the year. The pot of rice is cooked at home and brought to the community hall for the competition.

participate in the traditional rice cooking competition. At exactly at 11 AM, after a round of drum beating, the competition began with the following main stages[45]:

First: fire making competition, competitors rubbed the bamboo sticks to make fire with a bunch of straw. After that they made great efforts to blow into the bunch of straw to make the fire grow bigger to make the water in the rice pot boil, and they continued to do that until the level of water was just right.

They kept the rice pot in the fire for about 20 minutes until the rice was cooked evenly.

When the rice was cooked, the examiners put the rice into 4 bowls (one bowl from each team) to offer to the village Thành Hoàng, who had been General Phan Tây Nhạc under Hùng Vương the 18th.

After that, the 4 bowls of rice were brought to the outside of the community hall for public grading before the people and members of the 4 teams.

■ **Images of rice cooking competition in Thị Cấm village**

Preparing the rice pots   Hiding the pots in the ashes   Four bowls of rice offered to deity

Pictures of rice cooking competition in other villages

[45] All necessary things, such as rice, water, wood, pots, fire, were prepared by the organizing committee.

▪ Killing chicken, pig, and cow

The village meal jointly enjoyed by all village members is organized on the festival day on the occasion of the annual worshipping ceremony for Thành Hoàng[46] (called Kỳ Yên Festival in South Vietnam). On this occasion, there are killings of chicken, pig and cow, and the villagers are happy to make their contributions in money to be allowed to participate in the banquet, to obtain their parts of the foods, and to have an occasion to eat meat. The organization of the village meal is regulated in the village social contract.[47]

▪ Worshipped meal

The worshipped meal offered at the village community hall necessarily includes an alcohol container (Vô tửu bất thành lễ = Absence of alcohol negates the ceremony), a tray of cooked sticky rice, a pig or a chicken (raw meat animal),[48] fruit, and sometimes a special dish called

---

[46] For small banquets, for ceremonies for the 1st day (Ngày Sóc) and the 15th day (Ngày Vọng) of the month, or for the first day (Lễ Thượng Điền) and the last day (Lễ Hạ Điền) of the rice season, there was a limitation of participants ... For example, every month, on the 1st day and the 15th day, the elders offered a bunch of bananas, and a tray of betel and alcohol in the worshipping ceremony for the village god. After the ceremony, the offerings were divided into two parts; one half called "kiến viên" presented to the elders to enjoy, the other half divided into small pieces for everyone to share.

[47] For example, in the community contract of the Village of Phúc Xá, Province of Hà Đông prepared on May 15, 1923, Article 42, there is a statement regarding the main village banquet as follows: "Every year, on the 6th day of the 3rd month of the lunar calendar, people will organize a big banquet at the community hall with the participation of all village members, from the the elders to the adults of 18 years old and older. On that day people will kill cows or pigs, and organize musical performance for the worshipping ceremony. Nguyễn Thế Long, *Community halls and temples of Hà Nội*, Hà Nội: Culture and Information Publishing House, 2005, p. 392.

[48] A copious festival meal being "foursome" or "fivesome" depends on the custom of each village, for example, at Đình Bảng village the meal includes a dish of roasted rice field rat as "hèm"; at the festival of Hát Môn Temple, where the Trưng Sisters are worshipped, the meal always includes the dish of the vegetarian floating cakes.

«hèm[49]». As special characteristics of the meal, the pig offered must be a «*con heo toàn sinh* (still raw meat, and with its hair only summarily shaved off)», the cooked sticky rice offered must also be made with all purely white sticky rice. All of the worshipped objects should be carried to the community hall and received solemnly. The positions of the offerings during the worshipping ceremony should be corresponding with the social standings of the offering donors.

After the ceremony, the alcohol and foods become "sacred foods" to be shared among the villagers at the community hall or made into divided parts for everyone in the village. The people really cherish «*Miếng thừa lộc Thánh = The Deity's leftover*», and, thus, people used to say: «*Miếng việc làng hơn sàng xó bếp = One small piece of food at the village is worth more than a large portion of it in our kitchen*».

---

[49] Hèm is a habit of the deity, and sometimes it could be a bad habit, such as, thieving, begging; in these cases, the ceremony is organized indiscreetly.

Part 4
CULINARY CULTURE AND RELIGION

Within the Caodaist and Buddhist religious practice, following a vegetarian eating regime carries a very significant religious meaning for the spiritual life after death.

8

Vegetarian Meal
Symbol of the religious culinary culture

Eating a vegetarian meal is the eating of foods having been originate from plants, cereals, vegetables and fruit.[50]

The principal reason of religious characteristic of the practice of vegetarian eating within Caodaism and Buddhism is to keep the rules of prohibition: not to kill living creatures to avoid retribution in karma.

In Caodaism, vegetarian eating is a religious act determined in Caodaist dogma:

• Rituals: Before eating, the followers recite the orison «Kinh Vào Ăn Cơm[51]» (Orison Before Eating), and that is an act of "chánh niệm"[52] (Right Thinking), causing the rituals of eating become positive for the religious practice helping the foods we eat become **nutritional for both our body and soul**.

---

[50] Eating non-vegetarian meal is the eating of plants, vegetables, fruit and animals, birds, sea creatures as well.
[51] Kinh Vào Ăn Cơm (Orison Before Eating)
Giữa vạn vật con người một giống, (Animals and human beings are of the same origin,)
Phải uống ăn nuôi sống thân phàm. (Must eat and drink to nourish earthly bodies.)
Nhớ ơn bảo mạng Huyền Thiên,(We remember that our lives ae protected by Your Supreme Mightiness.)
Con mong mượn xác đoạt quyền vĩnh sanh. (We wish to borrow this body for eternal life.)
Từ bi ngũ cốc đã ban, (The cereals you have compassionately granted)
Dưỡng nuôi con trẻ châu toàn mảnh thân (To fully nourish your children's bodies.)
[52] Chánh niệm = Right Thinking: concentrated thinking on morality to reach one heart one concept.

After the meal, the followers recite the orison «Kinh Khi Ăn Cơm Rồi[53]» (Orison After Eating).

• Beliefs: Eating a vegetarian meal[54] is practiced because of our faith in the karma, and, thus, we do not kill living creatures in order to avoid retribution, and because of our respect for the law of birth and death, and also because of our practice to reach the state of Bi, Trí, Dũng (Compassion, Wisdom, Bravery): Not to kill living animals is Compassion; (Knowing that the animals would evolve into human beings is Wisdom; Refusing the temptation of drinking, passion ...is Bravery).

• Vegetarian eating is to reach the purity for our human body. Vegetarian eating is to keep Minh Thệ (Wow for Clarity), to keep Luật Đạo (Rules of Religion), in order to have a pure human body so that we can come across the many Tầng Trời (Levels of Sky) to rejoin The Supreme Being.

[53] Kinh Khi Ăn Cơm Rồi (Orison After Eating)
Nguyện nhớ ơn nông canh nhẫn nhọc, (We pray in remembrance of the hard work of farmers,)
Nguyện ơn người lúa thóc giã xay. (We pray in remembrance of people who processed the rice grains.)
Con cầu xin mảnh hình tráng kiện; (We ask for our bodies to be healthy)
Giúp nên công xây chuyển cơ đời. (So that we can help transforming the earthly life,)
Trên theo pháp luật Đạo Trời, (Up there, to follow God's Law,)
Dưới thương sanh chúng một lời đinh ninh. (Down here just one vow: to love all living beings.)
[54] According to Article 21, Chapter IV of Tân Luật (New Law).

1. Right way for vegetarian meal

It does not matter if the vegetarian meal is for disease prevention, disease treatment, or for religious practice, it should be done the right way, that is:

• We should eat many different kinds of plants, we should know how to coordinate different kinds of foods, we should know to change in accordance with age, with activities, we should prepare the meal carefully based on a nutritional balance to avoid an insufficiency of proteins, vitamins, minerals…

• A balance between yin-yang chi and the nutritional substances means that we should eat a lot of foods having yin-yang chi balance (greens, fruit, tubers, cereals…) and eat plants that are compatible with your potential chi state, and we should pay attention to foods having too much hot chi (like alcohol, hot spices… no good to hot potential chi state) or foods having too much cold chi (cold water, watermelon… causing diseases people having yin potential chi state)

• A balance between induction and consumption of chi under the form of calories, using scientific calculation of the number of calories needed for each activity, for each age… of each person.

• The foods should be in accordance with the religious ideal among co-followers, and at the same time should be delicious, having cleverly chosen tastes (fragrant greens, black and red pepper…), making the sour soup bowl really nicely sweet, and a dish of fried mushrooms really fresh…

Right way for vegetarian meal = balance between yin-yang and nutritional substances + wide variety + beliefs + interesting

The wrong way for vegetarian meal is:

• When the food chi are not compatible with the potential chi state. For example: the clinical symptoms of potential cold chi state (pale and cold body, low blood pressure, much urination, high heart beat, frigidity…) will increase if there is an abuse of yin chi foods such as watermelon, cold water, chrysanthemum tea, vervain…

• Eating not enough nutritional substances (protein, lipid, sugar), vitamins, minerals, resulting in a weak body, lack of physical forces …

2. Principles of vegetarian meal

Thanks to scientific progress, which have discovered all kinds of vitamins and nutritional substances, today those diseases caused by the lack of vitamins or nutritional substances do not result in fatalities like in the old days, but still can secretly cause harm to people if people do not pay enough attention and the nutritional chaos still can occur. Therefore, let me tell you stories of the fatal diseases or the incurable diseases of the old days caused by foods in order to show you the importance of the five principles of vegetarian meal as follows.

▪ Ăn rau trái, ngũ cốc toàn vẹn ở thể tự nhiên

In terms of chi, why should we eat plants in whole and in their natural forms? According to the concept of chi, each rice grain, each peas contains a volume of invisible innate chi, which is unchanged from the whole period of development from the grain to the big tree. Therefore, eating one whole pea or one sprouting pea means to absorb the whole volume of the innate chi of the full-grown tree.

According to this theory, eating a can of green beans or a can of sprouting alfalfa is equal to absorbing the innate chi of thousands of full-grown bean plants.

One example about the vitamins, how helpful is eating a whole brown rice grain? In 1878, Takati found the reason causing beriberi (weakened body, nervous disturbance, weight loss, paralysis, death...) in sailors because they have eaten white rice having no bran, causing the lack of Vitamin B1. In 1898, under the American influence, the Filipinos ate ground white rice and, thus, suffered from serious beriberi. They went back to eating brown rice and were cured of beriberi. The best way is to avoid or lower the eating of processed vegetable, fruit, and especially cereals. For example, rice will lose nutritional substance after each whitening processing.

▪ Vegetables and fruit should be eaten fresh and raw

How delicious it is to enjoy dishes of fresh-cut greens, and fresh-picked fruit! Fresh vegetables and fruit give us a variety of vitamins and minerals, especially Vitamin C. Do we get sick if we eat only foods lacking fresh ingredients, or over-cooked foods, or canned foods with loss of Vitamin C? In 1448, in a 10-month sea voyage with only salted meat and biscuits as foods, Vasco de Gama's expeditionary force of 160 sailors lost 100 of them when they reached the Cape of Good Hope. Because of lack of Vitamin C, the sailors suffered from scurvy (loss of teeth, swollen bleeding gums, internal hemorrhage, foot edema, and finally death). It was only up to the 18th century that Dr. Lindt discovered that the disease was caused by the lack of eating fresh vegetables and fruit.

Sciences also advise that we should eat fresh vegetables and fruit because of the observation showing that right after being picked the fruit begin to lose part of its nutritional substances, especially Vitamin C.

▪ Eating a variety of vegetables, fruit, cereals, and grains…

We should eat a variety of these foods to avoid a lack of nutritional substances, especially vitamins and minerals. From foods to beverages, no single one should be consumed regularly on a long-term basis because that case will end up with lacking this or that substance, and will result in certain disease. If people eat just only one or two kinds of foods (rice, corn…) they will get sick at some point in time. In 1740 in Italy, an unknown disease "pella agra" was discovered with symptoms such as dried skin, inflammation of mouth and four limbs, nervous disturbance, leading to craziness. The disease occurred only in poor people, who ate only corn and corn by-products. After they were allowed to drink milk, and eat vegetables and fruit, the disease disappeared.

▪ Eating foods with a variety of yin-yang chi

The basic principle of eating-drinking is the balance of yin-yang chi of foods by eating a variety of foods, which are compatible with the potential chi state. Dominant yang – weak yin, or vice versa, will lead to sickness. For example, if you have hot potential chi state, i.e., dominant yang, and you eat too much hot foods like alcohol, hot spices, mango, durian, longan… hot chi-related diseases, such as nose bleeding, hemorrhoids, high blood pressure, nervousness… will occur or be worsened. These diseases will diminish immediately after consuming foods having cold yin chi, such as cold water, sweet melons, watermelon, fresh vegetables and fruit, but at the same time you must also cut down the consumption of yang foods.

▪ Eating dried foods, avoiding drinking while eating

When eating dried foods, you should chew carefully, do not eat too much, which is very necessary for the digestion. While eating, especially for old people, try to avoid drinking cold water because the cold chi of water will lower the temperature of the hot chi in the stomach, creating some difficulty for the digestion, and, in the long run, could cause some harm to the stomach. For example, after you take some stomach drug fighting acid, and you still feel painful. The disease can be diminished or even cured (except for stomach ulcer, cancer, excessive anxiety) after consuming only hot foods and totally avoid all kinds of cold foods. Remember that stomach diseases will cause the absorption of vitamins and nutritional substances to diminish.

Therefore, with weakened body, or at old age, or being sick, we must revise our way of eating-drinking, eliminating bad habits or prejudices on foods, and listen to Albert Einstein's words: «*Nothing will benefit human health and increase chances for survival of life on earth as much as the evolution to a vegetarian diet[55]*» and give some thought to Einstein's lamentation: «*In this era, it is really sad that breaking an atom is easier than breaking a prejudice*».

5. Vegetarian meal and health

Everybody knows that a vegetarian meal can help people avoid a number of diseases relating to animal meat, for example, mad cow disease in humans (Creutzfeldt-jakob), bird flu, bad cholesterol. Eating much vegetables and fruit will prevent the development of arterial embolism, diminish the risks of cardio-vascular diseases, help the body retain several substances (pectin, beta carotene, lycopen, etc.), anti oxidants, and lowering the level of free radicals. However, people who eat vegetarian meal still can be sick if not paying attention to the following things:

- *Lack of nutritional substances, or vitamins, minerals because of old age, giving birth… will cause stomach weakness, resulting in a lower absorption of all substances;*
- *Abuse of food chi incompatible with potential chi state;*
- *Absorption of toxins caused by industrial processing.*

▪ Improvising in vegetarian meal

Therefore, the people who follow a vegetarian diet must know how to *"improvise"* if there are symptoms of nutritional disturbances like weight loss, tiredness, pale and frail body, weak action and motion… In these cases, if the doctor cannot find the causes, the first thing people have to do is to try to understand if the nutritional disturbances are caused by the wrong way of vegetarian meal, resulting in a lack of proteins, vitamins, minerals, or by the insufficient absorption of

---

[55] Albert Einstein has said: «*Nothing will benefit human health and increase chances for survival of life on Earth as much as the evolution to a vegetarian diet* »

nutritional substances caused by old age, pregnancy, gastro-intestinal diseases, or eating too much toxic chemicals...

If following a vegetarian diet and having a constant weigh loss, with a pale and weakened body, low blood pressure, and a deteriorating health ... often caused by the low volume of calories of the vegetarian meal, you should increase the volumes of the nutritional substances (by vegetarian meal, milk, eggs, vitamins...) in the following cases:

- *pregnant and lactating women,*
- *slow-developed children,*
- *old age, diminished absorption capability, resulting in lack of nutritional substances,*
- *after a serious sickness, in need of animal nutritional substances* (milk, eggs...)
- *people suffering from stomach ulcer, incapable of sufficient absorption of nutritional substances because vegetables and tubers contain too much gluten.*

If having those above-mentioned nutritional disturbances, the person eating vegetarian meal has to improvise, depending on which nutritional substance is insufficient. For example, if Vitamin B12 is insufficient he should drink more milk an eat more eggs, in case he follows the strict vegetarian regime then he can take Vitamin B12 or B complex. You should not practice vegetarian diet if your doctor or your nutritionist advise against it because of some disease like allergy to all kinds of beans, or grains...

▪ Insufficiency of substances

Protein[56]

Because of the limitation of the amino-acids the vegetarian regime follower must use a lot of vegetal proteins. Any vegetarian diet contains less proteins than the regular diet with meat, resulting in a

---

[56] Protein plays the main role in all the cells of the body. All enzymes are made of protein. Antibodies, hormones, bones all contain protein. Protein creates chi, helps moving the fat and vitamins, helps regulating the body's homeostasis. Protein is established by long twisting strings of amino acids, in which there is nitrogen. Our body contains 20 kinds of amino-acids, among which the body self-creates 11 kinds of them called non-essential amino acids. The remaining 9 kinds of them are supplied by foods and called essential amino acids. The symptoms of protein insufficiency are weight loss caused by weakened muscles, or easiness in getting colds, or feelings weak, etc.

lack of proteins and causing symptoms such as: constant tiredness, slow digestion, sluggish walking, lack of concentration, weak resistance to infection...

When these symptoms appear, people should increase their eating of foods that give much proteins such as: tofu, soybeans, lentils, Lima beans, rice, bread, peas, soy milk, all kinds of sesame, cashew, chestnuts, walnuts...

Comparison (100g), nutritional substances between soya milk and cow milk

	Soy milk 100g	*Cow milk* 100g
Water	92.5 g	87.0 g
Protein	3.4 g	3.5 g
Lipid	1.5 g	3.9 g
Sugar	2.1 g	4.9 g
Calcium	21 mg	118 mg
Phosphorus	47 mg	93 mg
Iron	7 mg	0.1 mg
Thiamine	09 mg	0.04 mg
Riboflavin	04 mg	0.17mg
Niacin	3 mg	0.1 mg

How much protein is needed? According to the RDA (recommended dietary allowance) for each person, the volume of protein needed for men is 60 grams and for women is 50 grams (American people). The calculation of protein for Vietnamese people must depend on age, body weight, climate, activities...

▪ Warning

Tofu and some other by-products of soybeans give much protein and help women at menopause become less fretful when their level of estrogen diminishes. However, women with too cold yin potential chi state (cold body, weak heart, much urination, diarrhea) should be careful because tofu contains much cold chi and could worsen their yin chi-related diseases. In that case, they should eat fried tofu in order to get more yang chi and less yin chi.

▪ Vitamins

Vegetarian meal could cause the insufficiency of vitamins, especially Vitamins B12 and D.

▪ Vitamin B12 insufficiency

Every day, our body needs about 3mg of Vitamin B12. According to scientific research, the people often have insufficiency of Vitamin B12 are:

- Women, who are pregnant and lactating at the same time, or will slow down the growth of the fetus. The symptoms of Vitamin B12 insufficiency, such as weak muscles, low vision, blood insufficiency, will disappear if taking supplements containing B12. In the old days in Vietnam, women having given birth could be paralyzed, and at night when lying down for sleep could feel a flow of cold air circulating in their bodies. Eating a bowl of bran will make that disappear right away, or, as of today, just taking one pill of Vitamin B12.
- The people who eat vegetarian meal on a daily basis often suffer from the insufficiency of Vitamin B12. Reason: Vitamin B12 exists only in foods from animals. A German research study discovered that 60% of vegetarian regime followers suffer from B12 insufficiency at level 3. At level 4, the nervous system could be damaged.
- Old people usually do not eat a variety of foods, or just eat a little, or suffering from chronic atrophic gastritis, leading to a decrease of the concentration level of hydrochloric acid and an increase of gastro-intestinal bacteria. The symptoms of the Vitamin B12 insufficiency in adults or old people are: memory loss, confusion, itchy limbs, asthenia, tinnitus,

blood insufficiency, un-balanced walking. From 60 years old onward, even people eating regular non-vegetarian meal can also suffer from B12 insufficiency. Reason: their stomach being weakened does not secrete enough gastric acid to digest foods, leading to B12 insufficiency in the liver and muscles.

▪ Vitamin D insufficiency

Every day, our body needs from 400 IU to 1000 IU. But according to recent research studies, many people are suffering seriously from Vitamin D insufficiency, and, thus, there is a need to perform blood test in order to determine the daily need, possibly increasing to 2 to 3000 IU. Vitamin D exists in large amount in sea foods, eggs, milk, and is created in the skin by ultraviolet rays (UV) of sunlight. Vitamin D helps moving calcium and phosphorus in the bone formation.

Symptoms of Vitamin D insufficiency: In adults, pain in the bones; in children, bone disease like rickets.

After 5 years of practicing vegetarian diet, if you do not consume eggs, milk then B12 insufficiency might occur, and the Vitamin D insufficiency might also occur if you live in countries with cold climate leading to not much exposure to sunlight.

▪ Zinc insufficiency

Zinc exists in animals and grains, cereals, and is very necessary for children's breastfeeding, during pregnancy, developing children because zinc helps in cell renewal.

A right vegetarian meal with a variety of foods will give all kinds of vitamins different from C, A, E and all needed minerals like iron, zinc, magnesium, calcium because all of these helpful substances are abundant in vegetarian meal foods like vegetables, fruit, greens, tubers, and nuts, and, thus, there are only two concerns:

• From 50 years old onward, the absorption power of the stomach gradually diminishes, and, therefore, we often

witness the symptoms of the insufficiencies of vitamins B, E, A, C, and minerals, especially magnesium;
• Even if you eat much vegetables and fruit, we still see symptoms of chemical insufficiency. Reason: vegetables and fruits are grown in barren land enriched by much chemical fertilizers, and, therefore, providing less minerals.

▪ Role of yin-yang chi of minerals

Minerals	Yin-yang chi	Daily needs	Insufficiency symptoms
Calcium	Yang	800 mg	Bone diseases, slow development
Magnesium	Yin	300 to 350 mg	Muscle diseases, muscle cramps
Sodium	Yang	3 to 5 g	Heart beating, low blood pressure, tiredness ...
Potassium	Yin	100 mg	High blood pressure, weak heart, nausea

▪ Warning

Warning no. 1: vitamin insufficiency

For a person with a normal relatively good health, only a blood test will tell us with certainty which vitamin is insufficient. Once the symptoms of insufficiency appear the insufficiency has become fairly serious you'd better take a pill for the insufficient vitamin but still must be careful of overvitaminosis.

Normally, we used to say I eat and drink adequately how can it happen. But we forget or do not know one thing: weakened internal organs do not absorb enough vitamins and minerals even when we eat adequate meals in the following cases:

• When people age, the internal organs also age. From 50 years old onward, sometimes the gastric acid is not secreted sufficiently to grind the foods in order to provide vitamins to our body; our skin also ages, and thus, recieves less sunlight leading to insufficiency of Vitamin D.
• Being pregnant, or breastfeeding a child, or being seriously ill all will lead to low absorption of all substances.

The solution is taking a blood test in order to take the vitamin we need; old people take additional multivitamins.

▪ Warning no. 2: minerals

Some religious organizations, in their teachings on vegetarian diet, often base on the Oshawa nutritional method of brown rice and salt + sesame, using the salty taste to clean acid... Nobody can deny the good and helpful things of this method; for example, one child, being too yin, Oshawa advised that giving him one spoon of gomasio (3/4 ground sesame +1/4 salt) will increase his yang chi, and the child will be happy. This method has cured many diseases, such as asthenia, eating too much foods containing toxic substances, yin-yang unbalance. During the time people practice this method, their bodies are resting, able to discharge the toxic substances, and become healthy. But the readers should be careful with some things about the teacher of this method:

• The lack of knowledge of yin-yang chi and of the nutritional science makes this method inflexible in its application of nutritional method. For example, it always advises using salt, and salted soy sauce without knowing that using too much salty taste will result in «water (kidney) and fire (heart) are incompatible,» causing some harm to people suffering from high blood pressure, heart and kidney diseases.[57];
• Lack of knowledge that the pair of minerals potassium (yin) / sodium (yang) is a pair of yin-yang chi. Abusing the salty sodium is creating the unbalance of yin-yang chi i.e. causing diseases;
• Sometimes books by Oshawa exaggerate that his method can cure all kinds of diseases including cancer, leprosy, smallpox, syphilis... Because of this exaggeration, many people believe these books and consider them as «oracles», and see no need for verification.

Therefore, for any advice or book on foods that does not help to better your health, does not help to diminish your existing diseases, and, on the contrary, cause new diseases, i.e. these things are not compatible with your internal organ chi state, then you'd better reconsider carefully.

---

[57] I have an old friend with high blood pressure that was dead by stroke because he believed in Oshawa method and continued to eat brown rice + salt and sesame.

4. Risks of chemicals in additives[58]

Toxic chemicals causing diseases could be contained in natural foods or could be derived from industrial chemicals used as additives to foods to add color, fragrance, or for preservation purposes. No matter they are natural or artificial, if used on a long-term basis, they are dangerous for our health.

▪ Natural toxic substances

Bamboo shoot (fresh or dried)[59] and cassava containing cyan hydric acid (used by the Nazis to kill people), if not carefully cleaned and eaten too much, could cause diseases like nausea, shortness of breath, headache… In fresh bamboo shoot, the bitter taste is the signal of the toxic substance. In order to diminish the toxic substance, we should remove the skin of the bamboo shoot, cut it into small slices and immerse them in salted water, then boil them 2 or 3 times to completely get rid of its bitter taste. In spite of all these precautionary measures, the toxic substance still remains in small amount, and, thus, we should not eat too much bamboo shoot and on a daily basis.

In the old days, the elders often advised that women should not eat too much cassava to prevent white discharge (Leukorrhea) caused by cyan hydric acid.

A number of tubers grown in the earth (Yin), will produce toxic substances when exposed to a yang chi-related environment. For example, potatoes,[60] exposed to light or sunlight, will lose Vitamin B and obtain a concentration of the toxic substance called solanine under the form of toxic blue spots that need to be eliminated before eating.

---

[58] See Appendix 3 : Interview of Professor Huỳnh Chiếu Đẳng by VOA on additives.
[59] The bamboo shoot flesh contains cyanuric compound (cyanogen), which, after being eaten, will release the very toxic cyan hydric acid (HCN) that can be fatal. Fresh bamboo shoot can contain 100mg HCN/100g, cassava about 40mg HCN/100g.
[60] Potatoes contain toxic glycoalkaloid, mostly in their skin. If placed outside, under the sun, their skin will become blue, a sign of the toxic solanine.

▪ Toxic additives in overseas processed foods

A number of ready-made vegetarian and non-vegetarian foods sold in stores often contain a too high concentration level of additives, and, thus, could cause a yin-yang chi disturbance or diseases if they are eaten too much and on a daily basis.

Monosodium glutamate (MSG). The phenomenon of abusing the MSG can become harmful if you always feel thirsty after eating the Vietnamese famous dishes, such as phở (North Vietnamese beef soup), bún bò Huế (Central Vietnamese Huế beef soup), suông (South Vietnamese ground-shrimp-balls soup)… or headache after having a meal at a Chinese restaurant (the Westerners used to call it Syndrome of Chinese restaurant). If you already have these symptoms and you continue to have «trưa hủ tíu tối cơm tàu = meaning Chinese vermicelli soup in the morning and Chinese dinner in the evening" then you'd better have to reconsider.

«"Tám" rice with fried pork sausage = Cơm tám giò chả». Pork sausages, fried pork sausages, pickled salted cucumbers and greens often contain too much MSG, sugar, salt, and especially the toxic borax, which will be harmful to liver, kidney, and sexual activity. We must stop the absorption of borax if we already have symptoms of weakened kidney (much urination, diminished sexual activity, prostate infection…).

Toxic substance in cooking oil. Tofu that is fried in cooking oil, which has been already used several times before, will become some toxic substance causing weakening of the liver and increasing the bad cholesterols (cholesterol LDL), one of the causes of heart attacks and strokes. Fat, used oil, coconut-milked oil, palm oil all contain saturated fat,[61] which will harm everyone eating vegetarian meal, no matter at home or in pagodas.

Traditional fermented bean curd requires several months in producing. To speed up the fermentation process, the producers immerse the bean curds in extremely strong acid before putting them in jars and have them fermented the next day.

Match salt, belonging to the nitric group, which is banned in the U.S., Canada,… is a carcinogen used in making sour nem, Chinese sausages in order to make these foods look nicely red.

---

[61] Saturated fat is found in animal products and processed foods, harmful to the heart because it increases bad cholesterols.

▪ Toxic additives in imported foods

The cooking of vegetarian meal or non-vegetarian meal always uses spices, especially soy sauce, oyster sauce, fish sauce. Many of these spices are manufactured in China, Vietnam and contain toxic chemicals.[62] Following are some examples.

▪ Toxic substances in soy sauce / soy paste

Food Standard Agency (FSA) announces that there are 22 out of 100 kinds of soy pastes are carcinogens. Reason: based on European food standards, some of them contain too much chemical food contaminant called 3-MCPD. 2/3 of kinds of soy sauces contain the chemical called 1,3-CPD, which should not be contained in foods. The following brands of soy sauce that should not be used: Golden Mountain, Jammy Chai, Pearl River Bridge, Lee Kum Kee, Wanjashan, King Imperial, Golden Mark, Sinsin, Golden Swan, Tung Chun, Kim Lan.

▪ Toxic substances in fish sauce

In the old days, when there were no chemicals in use, only salt and sunlight are used to preserve shrimps and fish. Now, people use the protein in the urea fertilizer to keep these shrimps and fish fresh for several days in boats before selling them to the fish sauce producing companies.

▪ Toxic substance Formol

Formol (gaseous formaldehyde soluble in water) is used in soaking corpses employed in the practice of medical students. The Chinese have taught Vietnamese people to use it in industry to keep fish from being rotted or to keep foods (rice noodle, vermicelli...) from being moldy.

---

[62] Please read this book: Peter Navarro, *Death by China: confronting the dragon: a global call to action*. Kindle Edition, USA, 2011 to know more about the toxic substances in foods produced in China and Vietnam.

I have personally done a test by placing a piece of frozen pangasius (also called shark catfish) produced in Vietnam, and a tilapia exported from China; after several months the fish were still not rotted, only hardened like wood.

Formol is also put in powder for rice noodle, rice paper, vermicelli to prevent them from getting moldy. In the 20 samples of rice noodles from Vietnam being analyzed, 16 of them have a fairly high concentration level of formol (Interview by Trà Mi with Prof. Huỳnh Chiếu Đẳng on VOA, see Appendix 3 at the end of this book). After having selected a brand of rice noodle or rice paper, you can perform a test by soaking it in water; if after a few days, it is still nice and hard like a piece of plastics, then you can conclude that it contains too much formol. Please think of this statement by Dr. Nguyễn Bá Đức of the Central Hospital for Cancer: «In Vietnam, every year, *there is an addition of 150,000 persons suffering from cancer, mostly caused by foods*».

▪ Toxic substances in foods

If you happen to see that the square rice cakes exported by Vietnam at the occasion of Tết have the wrapping leaves looking irregularly freshly green you should know that the producers have used batteries containing lead, mercury, arsenic, which are very harmful to our health.

Chinese dried mushrooms contain the insecticide made from carbon disulfide, and, thus, can be prevented from being moldy or rotted for several years. I personally did a test by placing these dried mushrooms in the open air for the whole year and they were still beautiful like at the beginning. Before cooking or frying them, we should soak them in water, then boil them, dry them up to get rid of all these chemicals, insecticides. The best way is eating fresh mushrooms, but do have some thought about the fact that in China and Vietnam many kinds of mushrooms are cultured in tanks containing chemicals.

When selected dried foods, we must pay attention to the fact that dried shrimps looking freshly red and not moldy are helped by the use of some kind of ant repellents (naturally dried shrimps by sunlight are blue-gray and easy to get moldy). Shredded pork skins are pure white because, by the Chinese "creative brain," they are cleaned with bleach.

«Vegetarian dishes faking non-vegetarian dishes»

Recently, in Vietnam, according to author Huỳnh Ngọc Thu[63], a Caodaist follower, the vegetarian meal of Caodaist followers has become much more varied «*with the appearance of vegetarian foods manufactured and imported from Taiwan, such as whole vegetarian roast chicken, vegetarian roast pork, vegetarian steamed duck, vegetarian beef, vegetarian pork... These vegetarian foods are bought by Caodaist followers from supermarkets, re-processed to use in banquets*». These vegetarian dishes faking non-vegetarian dishes "could" hide serious risks to health and religious practice:

- *They contain toxic additives for flavors, forms, colors, and preservation ...*
- *They even "could" contain animal meat* (causing the practitioners break their religious practice). *In 2004, the Taiwan press announced to the public the result of an investigation on these foods, which caused the death of a Buddhist follower, who had eaten vegetarian meal for 30 years. The doctor's diagnosis revealed that she was dead by eating beef infected by Creutzfeldt-Jakob disease in these vegetarian foods faking non-vegetarian foods, which included meat balls, fish balls, fish cakes, fish dumplings, and tempuras.*

In summary, the people cooking vegetarian or non-vegetarian meals should listen to the official advices published by laboratories on toxic substances in additives and in foods processed and produced in China and Vietnam. If we still have some doubts about these toxic substances in certain kinds of foods, we should test them like in the following examples.

Testing frozen fish, dried shrimps, white shredded pork skins... imported from China and Vietnam. If these foods contain toxic substances (Formol, bleaches...) then, even if we place them in the open

---

[63] Huỳnh Ngọc Thu, *Đời sống tôn giáo của tín đồ Đạo Cao Đài trong bối cảnh văn hóa Nam Bộ* (The Religious lie of the Caodaist followers within the cultural framework of South Vietnam) , 2010, page 162

air for a whole month, they will be much hardened but still looking good, not smelly, not rotted, not moldy; if we cook them with fish sauce, or roast them, or use them to make sour soup, the fish will be very smelly. When we test a brand of rice papers or rice noodles by immersing them in water for several days, and they still look nice but hard like pieces of plastics then we should know that they contain too much formol.

In summary:

Getting older, what observations do we have on health?

Observation from the classic oriental medical book, Huangdi Neijing, is that from 40 years old onward, the chi inside our body begin to gradually diminish.

Reaching old age, the internal organs become weakened, especially the stomach no longer does its job properly in grinding foods and absorbing nutritional substances; the skin of old people absorbs less sunlight to produce Vitamin D, and thus, told people often suffer from vitamin insufficiency, in spite of their proper and adequate eating, and their exposure to the sunlight for hours.

The good foods for our old age are selected by us. The good foods are the ones that are easily digested and could help us get to sleep easily.

The old people often exchange emails the sincere advices but not really based on medical knowledge, and, therefore, we should seek advice from our doctor before putting them in practice, for example, the advice to adopt the "cure-all" nutritional method of eating brown rice + sesame and salt for people have high blood pressure.

The people practicing vegetarian diet or religious places where vegetarian meals are prepared, but do not know which food ingredients or spices containing toxic chemical substances in additives, would be quietly causing harm, without their knowledge, to the people's health, leading to deadly diseases.

Conclusion for culinary culture

My reason to write about the culinary culture is to make a small contribution to help people know how to carry out the right eating-drinking and keep their good health, and at the same time:

- Reminding the readers of the traditional culinary culture, i.e., reminding the cultural identity of our people.
- Overseas, the Vietnamese language and Vietnamese foods are parts of our cultural identity, the two natural and easy-to-make factors in the preservation of the Vietnamese culture. One thing that we have observed is that, overseas, many children have forgotten the Vietnamese language but still keep many family habits, such as being very much fond of eating a number of Vietnamese dishes like beef soup (phở), Huế beef vermicelli soup (bún bò Huế), vermicelli with fried pork sausage (bún chả)… meaning that culinary culture is the most important factor in the preservation of our Vietnamese culture.
- In the survival of mankind, foods play an extremely important role like in the following advices:

«**First of all, use foods as medications**» (Words of Hippocrates, founder of Western medicine)

«**A good physician prevents diseass, a bad physician treats them**» (Words of the author of the classic Oriental medical book, Huangdi Neijing).

«**Foods and medications are of the same source**» (Words of Vietnamese Oriental medicine)

Lạp Chúc Nguyễn Huy
蠟燭阮輝

Appendix 1

The chi of fruit

All nutritional methods advise people to eat much fresh or dried fruit. Scientific analyses help us know which each kind of fruit providing the volume of which nutritional substance (water, vitamins, minerals, fibers…). In order to complement those scientific analyses, we present the invisible chi aspect of fruit and remind the reader that a number of fruits could create the yin-yang chi unbalance.

▪ Periods of chi transformation in fruit

Flower is the genital organ of tree, and, thus, has male pistil and female pistil, male flower (pistil containing powder) and female flower (pistil containing egg). The merging of male and female pistil will result in fruit.

From fertilization to ripening, the fruit goes through a non-stop transformation of its internal yin-yang chi through 4 main periods: fertilization, development, ripening, and withering. Let's take the examples of an orange, and a guava.

Fertilization period… When the fruit is still green, the yin chi is dominant (to help the fruit develop), and, thus, the fruit tastes sour or acrid (yin) and does not have much fragrance (yang);

Development period. The yin chi of the green fruit helps develop the physical part (weight) and also the essential substance of the fruit in the transformation to the ripening period;

Ripening period. When the fruit is ripe, that's the signal of the chi transformation has got to the highest point, expressed by:

• Its color changes to yellow, red (yang chi), and it tastes sour or sweet (yin chi);[64]

•The yin-yang chi reaches the balance, like oranges, peaches, grapes, apples… when getting ripe they have a light fragrance (yang) and taste sweet (yin), or transform from dominant yin (sour, no fragrance) to dominant yang (high fragrance);

Withering period. After the fruit becomes completely ripe, it begins to diminish in accordance with the yin-yang law. The diminution of chi leads to the withering of the cells, causing its skin and flesh to become gray, and its loss of fragrance; the fruit falls victim to the bacteria, and finally it is rotted and disintegrated, returning to the earth just like the human body.

▪ Transformation from dominant yin to yin-yang balance

In fruit, the chi transformation is observed through the change of its taste from acrid to freshly sweet, through its blowing fragrance, and through its color change at ripening. The readers can see this phenomenon of chi transformation in fruit like banana, guava, persimmon. When these fruits are still green, they contain much acrid-tasted tannin that will change its taste to sweet, and fresh (yin chi) and radiates its fragrance (yang chi) when they are ripe; it means that the inner chi have already reached a balance.

What observations does a banana give us? The green banana is hard and tastes acrid (signal of dominant yin) caused by tannin and starch. The green banana placed in-house or in tightly covered container, the tannin gradually disappears, meaning the dominant chi transforming into a yin-yang balance: the banana is ripe, becomes soft and sweet with some fragrance.

Banana eating way of Vietnamese people

We usually cook green banana together with yin chi animals like escargot, eel, and use the mixture in diarrhea prevention. The reason: the acrid taste of tannin has the effect of contraction of muscles and diminution of the secretion of organic liquids. In the countryside,

---

[64] In scientific terms, the changes of colors, flavors reflect the transformations of chemicals in the fruit cells.

after drinking too much alcohol, if feeling nausea and pain in the abdomen, people eat some green banana slices, and the symptoms disappear, thanks to the effect of the acrid taste of tannin.

On the contrary, eating ripe banana is very helpful, thanks to the yin-yang balance, the acrid taste of tannin (yin) having disappeared and left much potassium (yin), the starch becoming sweet sugar and providing much fibers. Therefore, green banana prevents diarrhea, ripe banana prevents constipation.

Persimmon (or Kaki)

Our elders used to say: *Number one custard apple, number two persimmon.* It is really wonderful to enjoy a fresh, ripening bright red persimmon. It is freshly sweet because it has already transformed from the state of dominant yin chi (acrid tannin) to the yin-yang balance (fragrant, red, sweet). Like the banana, the persimmon tastes acrid, even a little bitter, when it is still green because of the high level of tannin, which diminishes the secretion of organic liquid in the intestines, causing constipation or stomachache if we eat too much green persimmon and especially with its skin.[65]

Guava

Like banana and persimmon, the transformation of yin chi (acrid taste in tannin) to a yin-yang chi balance when the fruit is ripening (tannin dissolves and becomes potassium, giving out fragrance, and tasting sweet). We should only eat green guava to treat diarrhea (thanks o tannin) or stomachache caused by eating cold foods.

▪ Transformation from multiple yin to multiple yang: mangos, pineapples, durians

Fruit is sour when they are still green, and become sweet and fragrant when they are ripe, signaling the transformation of yin chi into yang chi, for example, mangos, pineapples …

Mangos

When the mango is still green, it is sour, with white or lightly

---

[65] Trái hồng, when still green, contains much tannin and pectin, which can merge with gastric acid and create gastric persimmon stones if we eat too much of it.

yellow flesh, signaling a state of dominant yin chi. When it is ripening, the yin chi transforms into dominant through its fragrance and its color yellow or red.

During their pregnancy, because of the needs for yin substances in nourishing the source cells of the fetus, Vietnamese women usually like to eat sour foods (yin) like green mangos dipped into a mixture of salt and red pepper (yang) for that reason.

The ripe mango with a string nice fragrance, with its flesh becoming fully yellow and very sweet, is considered as *"the queen of tropical fruit."* But you should be careful with this "queen" because eating too much mango while your body is of hot yang chi group you will suffer from the symptom of "dominant fire" causing hot skin, loss of sleep, sore reddened tongue…

Pineapples

The dominant yin chi of the green pineapple is detected through its very sour taste, not high in calories (52 calories / 100 g), but a lot of yin potassium (250 mg / 100 g). Just like the mango, when it is ripening the pineapple's yin chi transforms into yang chi, causing it to become nicely sweet, with its skin turning into dark yellow, a sign of the dominant yang chi. The process of transformation of the yin chi to yang chi continues even after being picked from the tree because the starch becomes sugar.

The green pineapple is used a lot in Vietnamese foods, such as sour soup, fried beef… Those people, who like to eat a lot of ripe pineapples, should stop eating them if having symptoms of *"bốc hỏa = blowing up fire,"* such as, skin reddened with pimples, uneasy dried mouth and tongue, blurring vision, nervous stomach, fast digestion, all caused by the hot chi of pineapples.[66]

In summary, the advice to eat much vegetables and fruit is a good one, but with the condition of eating a variety of them and paying attention to symptoms caused by the chi of fruit of just one kind of dominant yin chi or dominant yang chi.

---

[66] According to scientific explanation, it is because of the enzyme called bromelain, which destroys rapidly the protein, especially the animal protein.

Appendix 2

The culture in foods
(Written based on ideas of Hãn Nguyên Nguyễn Nhã)

In Vietnamese culinary art, our people do not prefer too nourishing foods; instead, we like to eat simple, delicate, healthy meal: fresh, not too much oil, nicely spicy foods that we can eat much, that we can eat to be full, but not too full, just to feel delicious, not too much nourishing to get fat: black mushrooms, pig ear cartilage, crispy pickled greens, we do not over-steam like the Chinese, and do not artistically display like the Japanese.

According to Hãn Nguyên Nguyễn Nhã, the Vietnamese culinary art includes 9 characteristics:

- *sociable and diversified*
- *not much oily*
- *richly spicy*
- *harmonious synthesis several flavors*
- *delicious and healthy*
- *using chopsticks*
- *community-related*
- *hospitality*
- *arrangement on tray with a common rice pot*

Poet Tản Đà's standards to have a delicious meal:

•*Delicious place*
•*Delicious tableware*
•*Delicious table companion*
•*Delicious foods*

Old concepts of delicious meal:

•*Quân tử thực lược chi vị* (Knowing that the foods are delicious would suffice for a gentleman)
•*Tiểu nhân sanh tử bất túc* (Eating until he dies would not suffice for a small-minded person)
•*Quân tử thực vô cầu bảo, cư vô cầu an.* (A gentleman eats without desire to be full, stays without desire to be safe)

▪ Regional characters

There are special products that are available only in certain areas, and, therefore, when you hear their names you know right away where they come from, for example, salted clam worms (mắm rươi), fried clam worms (chả rươi) are from the coastal area of North Vietnam delta[67]; salted sesamoidea (mắm ba khía) makes people think of Cà Mau mangroves; hilsa fish (cá cháy) reminds people of the brackish water region in Sóc Trăng; the tributed water spinach of Sơn Tây; the Đại Hoàng tributed banana of Hà Nam; and the Felica atria of the West Lake (sâm cầm Hồ Tây)…

All over the country, any village, any region, once becoming well-known for its special product or its famous dish, would be introduced in folk poetry, for example:

North Vietnam

cốm làng Vòng, (fried sticky rice nuggets of Vòng Village)
bánh cuốn Thanh Trì, (steamed rice rolls of Thanh Trì)
bánh Dì (dầy) *Quán Gánh* (ở Hà Tây) *có nhân đậu xanh giã nhỏ,* (Quán Gánh thick rice cake)

---

[67] The 20th day of the 9th month, the 5th day of the 10th month (lunar calendar)… we have "rain of clam worms" (mưa rươi) and "season of clam worms" (mùa rươi). The clam worms lay their eggs in the beach sands, in the coastal region of the North Vietnam delta.

in Hà Tây (with fillings made of ground green beans)
phở Hà Nội[68] (Hà Nội beef soup)
dưa La, (cucumbers of La Village)
vải Quang (lychees of Quang Village)
húng Láng, (mint leaves of Láng Village)
ngổ Đầm (ngổ greens of Đầm Village)
nem Báng, (nem of Báng Village; nem = fermented mixture of raw ground pork and shredded pork skin, made into squares wrapped with "vông" leaves)
tương Bần, (soy paste of Bần Village)
nước mắm Vạn Vân, (fish sauce of Vạn Vân)
cá rô Đầm Sét[69] (anabas of Đầm Sét)
Cốm vòng, gạo tám Mễ Trì, (Cốm Vòng, "tám" rice of Mễ Trì,)
Tương Bần húng Láng có gì ngon hơn (Tương Bần, húng Láng, nothing more delicious)
Vải Quang, húng Láng, ngổ Đầm (Vải Quang Village, hung Láng, ngổ Đầm)
Cá rô Đầm sét, sâm cầm Hồ Tây.(Anabas of Đầm Sét, fulica atra of West Lake)

Central Vietnam, land of the old capital city

yến sào Vĩnh Sơn, (swallow's nest of Vĩnh Sơn)
cua gạch Quảng Khê, (crab full of fat from Quảng Khê)
sò nghêu Quan Hà, (clam of Quan Hà)
rượu dâu Thuần Ly (strawberry wine of Thuần Ly)
ốc gạo Thanh Hà, (rice snail of Thanh Hà)
rượu thơm Hà Trung, (pineapple wine of Hà Trung)
mắm ruốc Cửa Tùng, (shrimp paste of Cửa Tùng)
mắm nêm Chợ Sãi. (Seasoned fish sauce of Chợ Sãi)
Xứ Quảng Qui Nhơn (Qui Nhơn, Quảng country)
Kẹo gương Thu Xà, mạch nha Thi Phố. (Peanut candy of Thu Xà, malt syrup of Thi Phố)

---

[68] Beef soup (phở) was originated from the village of Vân Cù, province of Nam Định; most phở vendors in Hà Nội were Vân Cù villagers (Nguyễn thị Bảy, Trần quốc Vượng, *Văn hóa ẩm thực Việt Nam (Vietnamese culinary culture)*, Từ điển bách khoa và Viện Văn Hóa (Encyclopedia and Institute of Culture), Hà Nội, 2010, p. 157)
[69] Village of La is in Hà Đông Province; Village of Báng (Đình Bảng) in Bắc Ninh Province; Village Bần in District of Mỹ Văn, Hưng Yên Province; Village of Láng in District of Từ Liêm, Hhà Nội; Vạn Vân, brand of fish sauce in Hải Phòng; Đầm Sét in District Thanh Trì, Hà Nội.

Sơn hào hải vị Khánh Hòa (Delicious mountain and sea foods of Khánh Hòa)
Yến sào Hòn Nôi, vịt lội Ninh Hòa, tôm hùm Bình Ba, sò huyết Cam Ranh. (Swallow's nests of Hòn Nôi, wading ducks of Ninh Hòa, lobsters of Bình Ba, cockles of Sam Ranh).

South Vietnam

Biên Hòa có bưởi Thanh Trà (Biên Hòa hasThanh Trà grapefruit)
Thủ Đức nem nướng, Điện Bà Tây Ninh. (Thủ Đức has roast nem, Tây Ninh has Our Lady Temple)
Bánh tráng Mỹ Long, mắm lòng Châu Đốc (Rice paper of Mỹ Lòng, salted fish intestines of Châu Đốc)
Cần Thơ chuột đồng, Bánh phồng Sa Đéc (Rice field rats of Cần Thơ, glutinous rice chapatti of Sa Đéc)
Gạo thơm Cần Đước, ba khía Cà Mau (Fragrant rice of Cần Đước, sesamoidea of Cà Mau)
Đuông nướng Đầm Dơi (Roast palm weevil larvae of Đàm Đơi)
Mắm còng Long An (Salted fiddle crabs of Long An)
Bò hóc Sóc Trăng (Prahok of Sóc Trăng)

Each country in the world has its own cooking art, but at the same time with common techniques and spice usages (steaming, cooking, cooking with fish sauce, boiling, frying, slicing, black pepper, red pepper, garlic…). Now, what unique characteristics does Vietnamese cooking art have? Based on our observations, there are four of them: 1) Using fresh fragrant greens as spices; 2) A wide variety of dipping sauces; 3) Auditory deliciousness; and 4) Folk medicine based on vegetables and fruit.

▪ Uniqueness 1. Delicate use of fragrant greens as spices

There is a wide variety of fresh fragrant greens, which cannot be absent in many of our dishes. The fragrant greens should be eaten fresh in order to enjoy the special nice fragrance of their essential oil, combined with the fresh delicious foods into a purely Vietnamese special product, totally different from other Asian foods.

Rau thơm, rau húng, rau mùi, (Fragrant greens, mint leaves, tasty greens,)
Thì là, cải cúc, đủ loài hành hoa. (Dills, crown daisies, and all kinds of onions.)
Mồng tơi, mướp đắng, ớt cà, (Vine spinach, bitter melon, red pepper, and tomatoes,)
Bí đao đậu ván vốn nhà trồng nên. (Quash, broad beans, all are home-grown.)

Many kinds of fragrant greens (mint leaves, parsley, perilla, fish mint, Vietnamese balm…), or fresh tubers, leaves, fruit (lesser galangal, turmeric, green banana, lemon leaves, piper lolot…), or fermented stuff (dried rice, liquid salted fish, pickles) are used as spices for food seasoning. For example:

- pig's guts should be eaten with mint leaves
- fake dog-meat dish with lesser galangal
- boiled chicken meat without fresh tiny pieces of lemon leaves
- pork seasoned with onion
- escargot noodle with Vietnamese balm
- spring roll with fragrant greens, or mint leaves
- balut with persicaria odorata (Vietnamese coriander)
- fake-turtle-meat-escargot with perilla
- fish-head sour soup with cilantro
- North Vietnamese fish soup with dills
- roast beef with piper lolot
- steamed escargot wrapped with ginger leaves
- steamed sticky rice wrapped with lotus leaves …

Therefore, we never forget the following ancestors' reminder:

Con gà cục tác lá chanh, (For the cackling chicken, get me the lemon leaves,)
Con lợn ủn ỉn mua hành cho tôi, (For the grunting pig, please buy onion for me,)
Con chó khóc đứng khóc ngồi, (For the standing or sitting crying dog,)
Bà ơi đi chợ mua tôi đồng riềng. (Hey, lady, go to the market and buy one dong of lesser galangal for me.)

Con trâu khóc ngả khóc nghiêng, (For the falling crying water buffalo,)
Tôi không ăn riềng, mua tỏi cho tôi. (I don't eat lesser galangal, so buy garlic for me instead.)

▪ Uniqueness 2. Art of making dipping sauces from fish sauce or salted fish

Just like the French cuisine well-known for the variety of sauces, one of the special characteristics of the Vietnamese cuisine is having a dozen of dipping sauces created from fish sauce, shrimp sauce, seasoned fish sauce. More special is the fact that these dipping sauces of the Vietnamese cuisine are prepared by the housewives themselves, and, thus, their flavors extremely varied, and, sometimes, even more delicious than the ones prepared in professional restaurants, while the French delicious sauces are prepared by the chefs and in accordance with formulas. These dipping sauces of the Vietnamese cuisine can be sour, sweet, hot and are all based on fish sauce or fermented salted fish.

▪ Dipping sauce for light foods

For pork sausage, people use pure fish sauce; for deep-fried anabas, people use Cự Đà soy paste; for rice roll pancake, people use fish sauce flavored by belostomatidae's body fluid; for spring rolls, people use just light fish sauce; for West Lake fried shrimp cake, people use sweet and sour fish sauce together with some pickled vegetables (papayas, carrots cut into threads and immersed in vinegar)…

▪ Dipping sauce for heavy foods

For the heavy foods, such as pig's guts, 7-course beef meal, hot pot, people use special dipping sauce made of seasoned fish sauce mixed with diced pineapples; for roast snakehead fish, people use tamarind fish sauce; for fatty foods, rice cakes, people eat them together with pickled vegetables (cucumbers, onions, …).

▪ Uniqueness 3. Auditory deliciousness

Why do Westerners have the custom of chin-chin glass clinking? In order for the ears also to enjoy the delicious foods, the Greek gods invented that kind of toasting during the meal. As for Vietnamese people, we try to find the sounds that could increase the auditory deliciousness in the culinary art, for example:

Chewing foods that emit audible sounds or give the feeling that the sound is in the mouth/. For example, people like to hear a pop when they bite a pickled garden egg (cà pháo); or people have the feeling of some sound when they chew black mushrooms, bamboo shoots, pig ear cartilage, crispy pickled cucumbers. When drinking the broth of hot liquid foods (phở, soup, pig-foot beef noodle soup...), we like to slurp it noisily so that we can really enjoy the foods; of course, we should avoid doing it in the presence of Canadian people because they consider it as not courteous.

After taking a sip of hot tea, we like to make a chirp;

When smoking a water pipe, people like to hear the hum since that makes them get high.

▪ Uniqueness 4. Folk medicine based on vegetables and fruit

Many spices have fragrances[70] (mint leaves, lemon grass, dill, ginger, cinnamon...), contain essential oils, i.e., yang chi, and a number of greens and fruit (pennywort, watermelon, lemon) contain much yin chi, and, therefore, after having eaten them, we feel fresh, cool. Thanks to the observations of the impacts of chi on their bodies, people advise one another about the chi state of foods, which one being warm, which one being cool in order to improve their bodies' temperature. Regarding those foods that are incompatible with one another, we have the following folk poem:

hịt gà kinh giới kỵ nhau, (Chicken meat and Vietnamese balm are incompatible,)
Ăn cùng một lúc ngứa đầu phát điên. (Eating them together will give a crazy head itch.)

---

[70] The odour through your nose is hot yang chi, the taste by your tongue is cold yin chi.

Thịt dê ngộ độc do đâu? (What causes the goat meat to become a food poisoning?)
Chỉ vì dưa hấu, chen vào bữa ăn. (It is because we also eat watermelon in the meal.)
Ba ba ăn với dền, sam, (Turtle eaten together with spinach, purslane,)
Bụng đau quằn quại, khó toàn vẹn thân. (You'll get terrible stomachache, very bad for your body.)
Chuối hột ăn với mật đường, (Pip banana eaten with honey or sugar,)
Bụng phình, dạ chướng, dọc đường phân rơi. (Your belly blowing out, your skin getting rough, you will suffer from diarrhea.)
Thịt rắn, kỵ củ cải xào? (Snake meat is incompatible with fried white radish?)
Ăn vào, sao thoát lưỡi đao tử thần (You eat it, you won't escape from death's sword.)
Nôn mửa bụng dạ không yên, (You get stomach disturbance and you vomit,)
Vì do hải sản ăn liền trái cây. (That is caused by eating fruit right after sea foods.)
Cá chép, cam thảo nhớ rằng, (You must remember that carp and licorice,)
Ăn chung, trúng độc, không cần hỏi tra. (Eaten together, will result in food poisoning, no need to ask.)

▪ Some differences from Chinese culinary art

a/ Regarding greens: Although they also eat boiled or fried greens, the Vietnamese people prefer to eat them raw while the Chinese people don't like to eat raw greens, raw vegetables and raw bamboo shoots.

b) Regarding fish: The Chinese people know how to cook with sauce, to steam, to fry like the Vietnamese people. They also have salted fish (khô, cá mặn) but not fermented salted fish (mắm) like the Vietnmese people. There are several ways to make fermented salted fish and eat them: **mắm thái** (mixture of slices of snakehead fish fillets + papaya flesh cut into threads + several kinds of spices) (ginger, lesser galangal), **mắm nêm** (seasoned fish sauce), **mắm ruốc** (fermented tiny shrimp paste), mắm tôm (ferment shrimp paste), etc. Other Southeast Asian countrues also make femented salted fish but they do not have many kinds of them like Vietnam

c) Regarding meat: The Chinese people know how to roast, cook with sauce, boil, fry, steam like the Vietnamese people but they do not know how to make nem, bì (mixture of fried pork cut into threads + shredded pork skin + spices) (garlic, salt, sugar, and ground fried rice grains), and chả lụa (cooked pork sausage), chả quế (cinnamon pok sausage), etc.

d) The Vietnamese people like salty and sweet; the Chinese people like sweet and sour.

Appendix 3

Additives
Interview of Mr. Huỳnh Chiếu Đẳng by Trà Mi (VOA – Vietnamese Program)

Mr. Huỳnh Chiếu Đẳng, a former senior high school teacher of Physics Chemistry, is a researcher and writer of several articles on food hygiene and safety.

Mr. Huỳnh Chiếu Đẳng. Additives are substances that are added to foods in order to give them colors, fragrances, or to preserve processed foods. From time immemorial, people have known to use additives like vinegar to immerse vegetables, leaks, like salt to preserve meat, fish, or color-producing substance like pandan leaves to create some fragrance and the color green, or the spiny bitter gourd giving the red used to make «xôi gấc» (spiny bitter gourd-flavored steamed sticky rice), or jasmine, lotus to season tea. All these substances can be considered as additives. But, lately, in industry, people use chemicals as additives for foods. Now chemicals are abundantly available for use by non-professional people. For example, using urea fertilizer to keep fish to be fresh for a long time is certainly something that should not be done.

• Trà Mi: There are two sources, first are the additives from the nature, and second are the additives from chemicals. Therefore, is it true that additives are not all unsafe, harmful for our health?

• Mr. Huỳnh Chiếu Đẳng: Additives are also necessary. Without them, it is almost certain that we cannot have canned food industries or ready-to-eat processed foods. Today, in all countries, we cannot find a single processed food that does not contain a bit of additives. Additives, if properly used, are indeed necessary. But currently, in those counties with recently developed food industries (like China, Vietnam), people are using very dangerous chemicals.

▪ Dangerous impact of formol

• Trà Mi: Sir, what additives are widely used, and we need to pay attention to?

• Mr. Huỳnh Chiếu Đẳng: This list is almost endless. But now, to cope with these additives, in countries already having experiences, like the U.S. or Canada, the government has established lists of chemicals used in foods; for those already in use for a long time and have not caused any effect, people call them «substances known to be safe.»

For example, the U.S. government has established a very long list, in which what substance is allowed to be included how much in foods, not too much. But currently in Vietnam, people use additives in very dangerous ways. On top is borax. This substance is not for eating, it is a chemical used in industries. For a long time, the Vietnamese people have used borax in bánh đúc (plain rice flan), giò chả (pork sausage), or in pickled vegetables to get them crispy. If we eat borax, even just a small amount, our liver, kidney, and genital organ could be damaged.

Another substance is also widely used by the Vietnamese people is saltpeter. In general, saltpeter is used for all substances belonging to the nitric group. In the U.S., saltpeter is completely banned, not allowed to be used in foods. But in Vietnam, saltpeter is widely used to create the red for pork. People use saltpeter in Chinese sausage and nem.

- Trà Mi: And, sir, what are the immediate and long-term dangerous effects of saltpeter?

- Mr. Huỳnh Chiếu Đẳng: The most dangerous effect of saltpeter that people have known is causing cancer. Of course, it's not like once in a while we eat a few pieces of nem or a pair of Chinese pork sausages and we get it. The importance is if we keep eating them day in, day out, this substance will be accumulated and will cause the disease in the long run.

Right now, people use formol to keep foods from being rotten. Formol is the gaseous formaldehyde dissolved in water. Formol is used in laboratories to immerse dead bodies of animals and plants, and, in medicine, to immerse human corpses for medical students' practice. As far as I know, in Ho Chi Minh City, 16 out of 20 samples of rice noodles, sent for analysis, contain formol with a fairly high concentration level.

- Trà Mi: We have heard that now even rice papers are also found to contain formol.

- Mr. Huỳnh Chiếu Đẳng: Yes, that's correct. I am very concerned about that.

- Trà Mi: What do they use formol for, Sir?

- Mr. Huỳnh Chiếu Đẳng: Formol is used to prevent rice papers from getting moldy. In addition to formol being used in rice papers, people also use bleach in them. The rice papers themselves are not white, not nicely transparent. But not only rice papers, even bean threads (bún tàu, miến) are very transparent because they also contain bleach.

In industries, bleach is used to clean the colors of those products that are seen as not nice. But in Vietnam, people use that substance in foods, and use it in a very risky way.

- Trà Mi: I'm sorry but I'd like to be a little more specific in my question: when people eat those foods containing formol, what harm do they get?

- Mr. Huỳnh Chiếu Đẳng: Formol causes cancer. Everyone knows about it for certain. According to Dr. Nguyễn Bá Đức of Bệnh Viện Ung Bướu Trung Ương (Central Hospital for Cancer), every year in

Vietnam there is an additional 150,000 persons with cancer, including 50,000 persons having the disease because of foods.

- Trà Mi: That's one-third.

- Mr. Huỳnh Chiếu Đẳng: Yes, one-third. And formol must be cited as one of the reasons causing that cancer situation in Vietnam.

▪ Urea fertilizer

- Trà Mi: In addition to formol, borax, bleach that you have just mentioned, the Vietnamese press has also recently reported that the urea fertilizer had been used in fish sauce.

- Mr. Huỳnh Chiếu Đẳng: The fishermen, working in the open sea, in order to keep the fish still fresh after several days on their boats so that they will still be sellable after they come back, have to preserve the fish with the urea fertilizer, i.e., a protein fertilizer. When this substance is absorbed into the fish bodies, it helps get them hardened and keeps them fresh for a long period. After having come back to the shore, the fishermen sell their catch to the fish sauce companies. These companies do not have enough water to wash and clean the fishes, but even if they do have enough water, they still cannot get rid of the urea because it has already been absorbed into the fish bodies. That's why the produced fish sauce still contains that level of concentration of urea in it. That is one reason.

Besides, I also know that people use «batteries» containing heavy metals like lead, mercury, cadmium, arsenic. These substances, contained in those so-called «batteries», are used to make the square sticky rice cakes (bánh chưng) look freshly green, or a number of other foods also look freshly green.

These substances are very dangerous, especially lead. Lead can harm the brain, especially children's brain. Next comes mercury. Cadmium is also a toxic substance, and arsenic is an extremely toxic substance, which was used to poison or kill people for a long, long time.

Recently, in the U.S., millions of children's toys were recalled because their coats of paint were discovered to contain lead. Paints mixed with lead have been used for a long time, and were called «sơn bạch diêm» (white-sulphurweed paint). The whole world has banned the use of lead for the past fifty or seventy years but the children's toys produced by China are still painted with lead.

Mercury is also a metal that people are very much concerned about. Pregnant mothers are advised to eat fish as less as possible

- Trà Mi: The bigger the sea fishes the more mercury they carry, is it true, Sir?

- Mr. Huỳnh Chiếu Đẳng: That's right. Mercury exists in the nature. The reason for fish to carry much mercury is the fact that the chemical plants have discharged it into the seas for the past several years, and that's why fish living close to the shore carry much more mercury than those living in the open seas.

These above-mentioned chemicals are usually harmful to the internal organs, especially the brain (by heavy metals), and then kidney, liver, and, of course, they make changes to the cells in the body, and lead to the final result: cancer.

- Trà Mi: The harms are such, but as you've just mentioned they occur only if these substances are used in big quantity and for a long time. My next question to you is: how much is considered as big quantity and how much time is a long time?

- Mr. Huỳnh Chiếu Đẳng: That depends on the substance used. For example, for borax the fatal concentration level is 15 g for one time use. That means with 15 g, it can kill an adult. For a child it is 3 g. But we never use that much because borax is not delicious at all. Secondly, when using it for rice papers, people also only use a very small quantity, and, therefore, when we eat rice papers, borax is accumulated gradually and the disease only occurs in the long run. This point is very dangerous because people would avoid the substances that kill immediately, but for the ones that do not cause any immediate effect, people are not scared and keep going on, and when the disease occurs it will be too late.

- Trà Mi: It's really a silent killer, isn't it?

- Mr. Huỳnh Chiếu Đẳng: Yes, it is. Therefore, in Western countries, the substances already known as toxic are absolutely banned to use in foods, not even a very small quantity. For example, this is the case of candies produced in Mexico. The Mexican producers did not use lead in their production, but lead was used in the soldering of machines employed in the production. The lead solder was dissolved in a very small quantity in the sugar, in the candies. After the candies are imported, the U.S. government analyzed them and found that very small quantity of lead, and immediately ordered their recall.

▪ MSG

• Trà Mi: For a long time, people have heard but have not believed completely the interesting information about MSG. Many people dare not use MSG in seasoning of foods because they have heard about its toxicity. What is the truth about MSG? Is it toxic or not, Sir?

• Mr. Huỳnh Chiếu Đẳng: The legend about MSG has existed for a very long time, for about twenty or thirty years. It has been the substance, to which I have paid attention the most, and, therefore, I know pretty much about it. It is just a legend. In fact, it is an additive that is almost harmless. I say it is almost harmless if we do not eat it in a large quantity. MSG is a substance that exist naturally in meat and fish, regardless we put it in or not. For example, when we do the fermentation of the soy sauce in the traditional way, MSG is already in there.

What is MSG? It is glutamic acid, which is a substance existing in meat and fish, i.e., in protein. It is also an amino acid, meaning it is a substance that exist in the nature.

In factories, where MSG is produced, people carried out the fermentation of cassava or, more recently, of fermentation of some other kinds of tubers. Some of the housewives avoid using MSG, but, in reality, if we go to restaurants, we will never be able to avoid eating MSG. I have a friend who works in a restaurant serving phở. He informs that for the large container of phở broth, people use 2 packages of MSG, sometimes even 3 packages. Each package weights half a kilogram. Therefore, when people come home, after having eaten phở in a restaurant, sensitive people will feel their mouth dried up, a little bit dizzy, and some numbness in the tongue. Some other people get itchy in their skin too. These people are known to be allergic to MSG. Statistically, 1 in 100 persons is allergic to MSG, a phenomenon called «Chinese restaurant syndrome».

- Trà Mi: Is it correct that the immediate effects that scare people?

- Mr. Huỳnh Chiếu Đẳng: Yes, that's correct. Anh that symptom is called «Chinese restaurant syndrome» by the Americans because in general, in all Oriental restaurants, by competition, people always use MSG. If you do not add MSG (to foods), the clients do not feel that the foods are delicious. But the restaurant owners and their clients as well do not know that MSG create more flavors, it increases the sweetness of meat and fish. Also, they do not know the flavors increase has a limit, beyond which it does not matter how much more MSG you put in, there is no more flavors increase. That's why you should not use too much MSG in your cooking. Beyond that limit, MSG is no more useful. It is incorrect if f we say that MSG is totally unharmful, but MSG is a safe additive and already known for certain that it does not cause any disease in the long run. The U.S. government, however, has recommended that pregnant women and infants should not eat foods containing MSG. I also know that, in the old days, French people use MSG as a nourishing substance for the brain. When we were young, still in high schools, we used to take these brain-nourishing pills. These pills were glutamic acid. The French also produced that medicine under the form of liquid, or in ampoules and called them glutaminyl. If MSG were a substance that could cause disease in the long run, the French would know and would not have used it like that.

- Trà Mi: Rumors have been circulated that MSG is produced from toxic industrial cassava, and, therefore, people are afraid that MSG's quality is not guaranteed.

- Mr. Huỳnh Chiếu Đẳng: Yes, cassava is toxic. It is not toxic because you eat it. Cassava, especially its leaves and its flowers, contains a kind of acid called cyan hydric acid. This acid was used by the Nazis to kill the Jewish people. Today, there are still some places where people use that substance to execute prisoners already sentenced with death penalty. here is a small amount of cyan hydric acid in cassava, just like in bamboo shoot. If we boil cassava with too little water or we eat the cassava sprout we could suffer from some poisoning caused by that acid. But if cassava is boiled with much water or we let cassava powder get fermented and become MSG then there is nothing to do with cryohydric acid any more. MSG is fermented by the yeasts living on cassava, not by the cassava itself. Therefore, eating boiled cassava sprout can get you poisoned. The same thing happens if you eat bamboo shoot without having it boiled two or three times

▪ All kinds of fermented salted fish

• Trà Mi: Now I'd like to ask you about one traditional food that is very much popular in Vietnam, very familiar with everyone, and that is the fermented salted fish (mắm) of all kinds. For many Vietnamese people, mắm is enjoyed just like other delicious mountain and sea foods. But today people have some doubt about the fact that even mắm also contains toxic additives. Is it true, Sir?

• Mr. Huỳnh Chiếu Đẳng: Thank you for asking this question. Yes, I'd like to talk a little bit about mắm. Mắm, made by our ancestors in the days, itself was very toxic. The American USDA advises their people that when they travel to foreign countries like China or other Asian nations, they should not eat salted proteins. The U.S. government meant that they should not eat salted meat, salted fish, i.e., mắm, khô (dried salted fish), and salted vegetables. If I remember correctly, even the Chinese government also advised their people not eating too much salted vegetables. Salted and pickled vegetables have been the traditional foods of the Chinese people. And the Chinese government knows that they cause cancers. Now, let's go back to mắm. First, mắm itself is salted protein that includes many toxic substances considered as carcinogens in the long run. Second, mắm contains too much salt. According to professionals, an adult can only take in from 1 to 5 g of salt a day. This is a very small amount compared to the amount of salt that the Vietnamese people take in a day now.

Even for the European people, based on French statistics, the volume of salt they take in every day is already 5 or 6 times the limit of 1-5 g. And people know that with that daily level of salt take-in, cardio-vascular diseases will occur.

Therefore, the level of fermented salted fish, and fish sauce we consume daily now is already too bad. But currently, people also add to mắm several additives that we cannot control. These are the initiatives of the producers, they add whatever they want, just to make the foods look fresh, good, nice, delicious and people would eat them.

I also know that the dried fish (khô), like the dried net Uma thalassemia (khô cá thiểu), based on a reportage that I have read from some newspaper published in Vietnam, people use some kind of non-tasty sea fish, have them ground and them mixed them with too much of some kind of additives. After that, they pressed them into pieces looking like dried net uma thalassemia, and dried them in the sun. According to that newspaper correspondent, when they dried them like that, even the flies dare nor get in touch with these pieces. We really should worry about that.

I've also learned that the dried shrimps were sprayed with ant repellent to keep them from ants, from being moldy, and looking fresh too. I don't know what kind of substance used in that ant repellent, but, if even the ants won't touch them then people should not touch them either.

▪ Dried squid and all kinds of dried fish

• Trà Mi: What about dried squid? And other kinds of dried fish, should we be concerned about them too, Sir?

• Mr Huỳnh Chiếu Đẳng: Up to today, I don't know what substance people use for dried squid, but I know that the squid itself has a high concentration level of cholesterol. Dried quid is one of the foods with the highest level of cholesterol. Next come pig brain, and ox brain.

• Trà Mi: Although without food additives, Sir?

• Mr Huỳnh Chiếu Đẳng: Yes, even without additives. But it is not good to eat too much dried squid, because of its very high level of cholesterol. It is even higher than in egg yolk.

- Trà Mi: Yes. Today, cholesterol is something to be scared of.

- Mr. Huỳnh Chiếu Đẳng: It is something that we are advised not to bring too much into our body. The daily in-take of cholesterol recommended by the USDA for an adult is less than 300 mg. One chicken egg yolk contains from 250 to 300 mg. Duck eggs contain a lot more cholesterol than that.

Appendix 4

Royal banquets under Nguyễn Dynasty

Tôn Nữ Thị Hà & Phan Tôn Tịnh Hải

There were meanwhile some patriotic men of letters, like Nguyễn Trãi, drank tea called "tước thiệt" (sparrow's tongue), a kind of precious tea of Nghệ An, with leaves as small as the tongues of sparrows, and drank it at "thạch bàn" (stone table) on Côn Sơn mountain, not in house like "trà thất" (tea room) in China or Japan.

When you get to the royal palace, you enter some noble, majestic, and huge space; when you get to the royal banquet palace, you will be overwhelmed by the luxury and magnificent of the gold-plated tableware and the extremely and especially fussy dishes.

▪ EIGHT PRECIOUS DISHES AS NATIONAL TREASURES

When all guests have already taken their seats in accordance with their rank in the palace, the emperor's palanquin with all accessories like fans, flags, parasols, canopies started moving from Càn Thành Palace to Cần Chánh Palace. Inside the palace, the head of the royal guards yelled: "nội tế" (Inside, prepare!), outside the palace, a military mandarin yelled: "ngoại chỉnh" (Outside, get ready!). When the emperor arrived at the palace's gate, the head if the royal guards yelled: "Thánh thượng giá lâm, chấp sự giả cát tư kỳ sự" (Nhà vua đã đến, ai lo việc nấy; His Majesty Has Come; Everyone, Carry Your Duty!). After the ceremonious procedure for the emperor 's secure sitting for the banquet, the head of the royal guards offered him his first glass of one-hundred-day-wine ("Nhất bôi tửu bách nhật") and the evening sumptuous royal banquet began.

Right at this moment, the palace musical band started playing the song praising the emperor's achievements. With high noble tone in melodious rhythm, the song included the following beautiful lyrics: *"Vũ đài xuân rạng hàng ngũ chỉnh tề, sân khấu mây lộng âm thanh dìu dặt... Khánh chuông ra lệnh xướng hòa, kèn trống nhịp nhàng đánh thổi... Trải mấy triều vương đều khuyến khích. Biết bao âm nhạc thầy dồi dào... Giữa điện đình ca múa, tô điểm thái vận nước nhà. Trên lăng miếu xướng hòa, ngưỡng đức cao thâm biển núi"...* (Translation from Sino-Vietnamese words into Vietnamese language by Ưng Dự). (Translation into English: "The spring stage is shining with blowing clouds in the background, with slow, soft, and rhythmic sounds and with all dancers ready... Bells and cymbals are giving orders to rhythmic choir, and to trumpets and drums to start playing... Encouragements have been given throughout all dynasties, leading to rich and diverse music... The singing and dancing right in the middle of the palace are showing the stable and prosperous conditions of the county... Within the royal temples and palaces, music and chants are melodious and harmonious, revealing our respects for the emperor's achievements that are as great as seas, and as high as mountains.)

On the banquet table, the second glass of wine ("Nhị bôi tửu") (huỳnh tửu = yellow wine), non-vegetarian foods, 16 plates of cakes and fruit, 16 plates of sweets, were respectfully arranged, all nicely fragrant, and beautifully prepared in form of the four sacred legendary animals (dragon, unicorn, turtle, and phoenix), and ready to serve the emperor and the mandarins.

Peacock nem (nem = common name for fermented mixture of ground pork shredded pork skins) is one of the most distinct dishes on the banquet table, being prepared by a very sophisticated but effective way. This food is self-cooked by the microbial fermentation caused by the interaction between the hot spices, such as, galangal, garlic, black pepper, with sugar, and ground peacock thigh meat. The selection of the thigh meat was considering as a professional secret of the Lý Thiện (the cook team in preparing royal banquets), which would make nem fragrant and sweet without using sugar or MSG. Peacock nem was considered as the guardian angel of kings because of its capability of detoxification in case of light food poisoning. In addition, the Lý Thiện team also prepared the phoenix meat sausage, which was not fried but wrapped in banana leaves and steamed.

The rhino skin was very thick, therefore, in the old days, people only took its armpit skin, the thinnest part, immersed it in water to have it softened, and then cooked it before eating. Another exquisite dish, which cannot be absent on the banquet table, is the swallow's nest sweet soup, which was sometimes cooked with lotus seeds; and some other time, the swallow's nest was stuffed in pigeons and steamed. The emperor only offered swallow's nest dishes to the ambassadors of foreign countries and to new top graduates of examinations.

Swallow's nest sweet soup

The deer tendon dish reflected the ultimate food selection of kings. In order to obtain the tendon part, the deer thigh must be burned on fire, shaved to remove all hair, and then boiled until the meat became tender. After that, people used a pointed knife to separate the tendon part from the muscles, and immersed it in water (mixed with salt and vinegar) to have it whitened. In the meantime, a whole chicken was steamed to obtain the sweet and limpid broth after removing all the fat. The broth was then used to steam the deer tendon already cut into pieces, together with dried shrimps, bamboo shoots, all kinds of tubers and beans, and pork sausage. When everything was softened then it was seasoned.

According to the legend, gorilla's lips, bear's paws, elephant foot tendon, were all ingredients of delicious dishes, which could not be imitated, but their cooking techniques were almost lost.

▪ ARTISTIC DISPLAY

The artistic sophisticated display of dishes, combined with the extremely skillful culinary art of the chefs in the Thượng Thiện và Lý Thiện teams have always pleased the most difficult kings. These delicious dishes were presented beautifully and cleanly. The banquet table was always full of different colors and flavors, which were intertwined harmoniously, no single color being dominant, and no single flavor dominant either. The art of mixing colors (from fruit to plants to vegetables) also reflected the ranks of artisans working in the royal palace.

The banquet was well-known not only because of these delicious mountain and sea foods but also because of the rice from An Cựu, which had been selected grain by grain, and cooked in earthen pot with no-flame fire in order to obtain the plump, soft, and unbroken rice grains. Every time the rice was already well-cooked the whole area of the royal kitchen was overwhelmed with nice fragrance; and the earthen pot was destroyed, so it would never be used a second time.

In addition to these delicious foods available only in these banquets, the following special and exquisite foods, such as, fried fish balls, roast whole chicken, tiger shrimps, goat meat, pig stomach, steamed whole chicken, horseshoe meat, roast pork, steamed pig foot, vinegar duck, steamed whole duck, steamed white pigeon, steamed pork, roast goose, pork sausage, spring rolls, roast duck, sliced chicken, red steamed sticky rice, roast rice paper, grey steamed sticky rice, were added to the banquet menu. From these 50 bowls and 16 plates, just one piece picked by the chopsticks would help the guests feel completely full.

▪ TEA AND WINE AT END OF BANQUET

The third glass of wine ("Tam bôi tửu") (orange-peach wine) was offered to the emperor to help neutralize the remaining flavors of more than 30 previous dishes, and to obtain the balance with the up-coming 20 dessert dishes. In addition to the fruit, there were the following dessert dishes: sweet soups, a wide variety of cakes (bánh lá gai = spiny leaf glutinous rice cake, bánh tiến đôi, bánh uyển cao, bánh bột vàng = yellow-flour cake, bánh bột 5 màu = 5-colored-flour cake, bánh trứng gà = chicken-egg cake, bánh bao = pork bun, bánh bột sắn trắng = white-cassava-flour cake, bánh bột sắn vàng = yellow-cassava-flour cake, bánh phồng = puff-pastry cake, bánh hình củ gừng = ginger-tuber cake, bánh trứng sẻ = sparrow's egg cake, bánh rán vừng = sesame-deep-fried cake, bánh thạch hoa= stone-flower cake), and several kinds of dried sweetened fruit (mứt, such as mứt gừng = mứt of ginger, mứt báo bão = mứt of storm-warning, mứt tứ linh = mứt of four sacred legendary animals, mứt màu hoa = mứt of flower color, mứt màu quả = mứt of fruit color, mứt táo = mứt of apple, mứt dưa = mứt of melon), a plate of azarole fruit, and dried watermelon seeds.

Now of all these dished on the banquet table was just simply placed there. All of them were very subtly displayed, requiring a time-consuming and painstaking cleverness. Each kind of cake might require up to 4 days to prepare and make, and, unfortunately, many of these techniques have been lost.

After the emperor and the mandarins have satisfactorily enjoyed these dishes here came the important part of tea enjoyment. There are many kinds of jade tea offered to the emperor, such as the lotus tea with a very nice fragrance because it was wrapped with lotus leaves together with lotus flowers. The lotus fragrance was absorbed into every single tea leaf and, thus, when the tea was poured out its fragrance deeply impacted one's olfaction. The Nguyễn emperors specifically liked to enjoy the tea flavored with magnolia or cholorantus. The tea was boiled in small pot, and then these flowers were immersed in, causing the unforgettably passionate fragrance. Made by the same technique, we also have climbing-rose tea, golden-chrysanthemum tea The lightly-shaking-colored climbing-rose tea was nobly beautiful, while the golden-chrysanthemum tea, producing a nice freshness, was a favorite tea for summer.

Lotus tea

The Nguyễn emperors from Minh Mạng onward usually offered royal banquets to royal family members, princes, mandarins (both administrative and military), and ambassadors … in Cần Chánh Palace. From Emperor Khải Định's reign, the banquets were organized in Kiến Trung Palace (at Minh Lâu Viên); later, sometimes, Emperor Khải Định also organized the banquets at An Định Palace, his own palace located on the An Cựu River's bank.

The emperor took his seat on the golden-edged mat, on which was placed a tea table and a 5-leafed-back-support pillow. In front of the emperor was another table containing his daily stuff like his water-pipe, the bell (on a hanger for him to strike when he wanted to call the servants), the round bronze betel container, the spittoon, the tea tray, and the wine bottle. That was the place where the emperor sat to enjoy his meals, nobody was allowed to sit there with him.

The emperor worn his crown embroidered with image of two dragons fighting for a pearl, his Nine-Dragones Yellow Royal Robe, with all his personal accessories like scarf and belt, the ivory scepter, and his boots. When the emperor was already secure in his seat, the guards removed and safeguarded the crown, the scarf and belt, the scepter and the boots. The emperor kept his Yellow Royal Robe, with a yellow headband (in form of the letter Nhựt meaning the Sun), and wearing only socks to attend the banquet.

In front and behind of the place where the emperor had his meal there were hangings and curtains; on the columns there were wooden plaques bearing parallel sentences. On both sides, there were hangings made of wood or brocade, a number of porcelains stands holding the pot of artificial trees having jade leaves and golden branches, two shelves for royal armory, one shelf for the wash-hand-basin, and two shelves for the big fans. In order to make the scene more magnificent, under the ceiling there was a brocade Nine-Dragon-embroidered parasol, with a crystal candle chandelier together with Four-Sacred-Legendary-Animals lanterns creating the warm feelings of prosperity and authority.

The sitting place for the mandarins included several rows of tables, arranged into two opposing lines. The royal guards indicated seats for the mandarins in accordance with their ranks, no one was allowed to sit in front and opposite to the emperor. The ambassadors wore their solemn national costumes. The mandarins, wearing brocade robes in different colors (except yellow), and turbans (except letter sun turban), carried ivory tags with indication of their rank.

The royal guard team serving the emperor was consisted of the head taking care of the general responsibility, and eight members responsible for specific duties. Each banquet table had two guards taking care of the fanning, two guards taking care of the parasol, two guards taking care of the food serving, one royal physician, one mandarin form the Directory of Imperial Observatory (quan khâm thiên), one military mandarin for the protection (military mandarin was not allowed to sit at the banquet table); the mandarins represented the emperor to take care of the guests.

All great banquets were regulated to include 50 bowls and 16 plates. In order to have as much food ingredients for these dishes in the menu, a hunting team (called Vệ Võ Thành) was created. In Minh Mạng 7th year (1826), the emperor ordered the team keep a group of 100 hunting dogs for use only in the hunting. Every year, 12 days before the death anniversaries, 300 members of the hunting team must carry out the hunting of wild animals, and for each time, they had to come back with at least 10 animals.

The unit responsible for the emperor's meals was established during the reign of Emperor Gia Long (1802) and called Thuyền nội trù. At the beginning of the reign of Emperor Minh Mạng, it was renamed Thượng Thiện Đội, which was consisted of 50 persons (1820); each person was responsible for one dish in abondance with his specialty. Besides, there was another unit called Lý Thiện Ty specializing providing exquisite dishes, Tả Chuyên TY specializing in making cakes, sweets, beverages, Hữu Chuyên Ty responsible for providing services. All of these specially sophisticated responsibilities are aimed at providing the absolute delicateness of the culinary art in servicing the royal banquets.

Appendix 5

Plants through Vietnamese poetry
Professor Thái Công Tụng

INTRODUCTIONL. *Professor Thái Công Tụng, former professor of several universities in Vietnam, has authored many valuable books and research studies on Vietnam. After his retirement as a specialist from ACDI (Agence Canadienne du Développement International), Professor Thái Công Tụng, currently residing in Montreal, Canada, continued his research and creative work. His most recent book,* **Việt Nam văn hóa và môi trường** *(Vietnam: culture and environment) was published by the Institute of Vietnamese Studies (Viện Việt Học) in California.*[71] *With Professor Thái Công Tụng's agreement, I hereby introduce a section in one of his research studies for your reading.*

In the world of plants, and more specifically in agriculture, we can cite food plants, plant giving fibers, vegetables ...

Food plants include: cereals, plants giving tubers, plants giving beans, nuts.

Cereals include: corn, sorghum, wheat, malt, rye (seigle in French), barley (orge in French), oat (avoine in French), and rice. **Corn**, originated from Central America, and later introduced into Asia, is also an essential food plant. **Sorghum**, also called coax seed (bo bo), looks like corn, or millet.

---

[71] If interested, readers can contact dolehuong@gmail.com or Amazon to buy.

Rice also has several species:

Vụ chiêm em cấy lúa di, (In the dry season, you plant the di rice,)
Vụ mùa lúa dé, sớm thì ba giăng. (In the main season you plant dé rice, if earlier you plant three-moon rice.)
Thú quê rau cá đã từng, (We have enjoyed the countryside's vegetables and fish,)
Gạo thơm cơm trắng chi bằng tám xoan. (No white and fragrant rice can beat tám xoan rice.)

There are two main kinds of rice that people plant: 1) The regular rice (lúa tẻ = tẻ rice) producing the non-sticky rice that people cook and eat at their daily meals; rice flour is used to make many products such as vermicelli (rice noodle), rice paper, steamed rice rolls. 2) The sticky rice, with its soft grains, is used to make steamed sticky rice (xôi), square sticky rice cake (bánh chưng), cylindrical sticky rice cake (bánh tét), sticky rice wine, and rice wine (cơm rượu), etc. In folk poetry, these two kinds of rice are subjects of love between boys and girls:

Anh thưa với mẹ cùng cha (I have asked mt mother and my father)
Nếp mà lộn tẻ, lựa ra hay đừng? (Sticky rice mixed with regular rice, should we separate them or not?)
Đò đưa đến bến đò ngừng (Having reached its destination, the ferry would stop)
Anh thương em thuở trước, nửa chừng lại thôi! (I loved you in the past, but I stopped at mid-way!)

The rice plant has many different development periods: it is called cây mạ (rice seedling) when still young, then it multiples itself, then it blossoms (trổ đòng đòng), and finally it produces grains:

Anh đi lúa chửa chia vè, (When I left, the rice has not multiplied yet,)
Anh về lúa đã đỗ hoe đầy đồng. (When I came back. the rice has already blossomed all over the field.)
Anh đi em chửa có chồng, (When I left, you were not married yet,)
Anh về em đã tay bồng tay mang. (When I came back, you were already so busy with your children.)

Plants giving tubers, such as: sweet potato (khoai lang, *Ipomea batatas*), cassava (khoai mì, *Manihot esculenta*), taro (khoai sọ hay còn gọi là khoai môn, *Colocasia antiquorum*); its tubers are edible, its petiole can be pickled; khoai nưa (*Amorphophallus rivieri*) of the same family Ráy (Araceae) like toro, its tubers are also edible but causing from itch, khoai nước (*Colocasia esculenta*), also called môn nước, birth tuber and petiole are edible, yam (khoai từ, *Dioscorea esculenta*) widely grown in many villages.

Plants giving beans / peas such as: soy bean (đậu nành also called) đậu tương *Glycine max* (of the Fabaceae family), containing much protein, can be used to make tofu, bean curd, soy sauce; cowpea (*Vigna unguiculata, of the* Fabaceae family); black bean (*Vigna cylindrica*), often used to make sweet soup that helps digestion and suppresses heat; green peas (đậu Hà lan, *Pisum sativum*) of which young fruit and nut can be edible; Lima bean (đậu ngự, *Phaseolus lunatus*); broad bean (đậu ván, *Dolichos lablab*); green bean (đậu xanh, *Phaseolus aureus*), used to make bean sprout (giá), used to make chopsuey; dwarf bean (đậu lùn, (*Phaseolus vulgaris*),. In some regions we also have pigeon pea (đậu triều, *Cajanus indicus*).

In addition to food plants, there are several kinds of greens (rau). Talking about greens, we have the following folk poem:

Ai đâu mà chẳng biết ta (Who does not know me)
Ta ở Xóm Láng, vốn nhà trồng rau (I live in Láng Quarter, from a family specializing in growing greens)
Rau thơm, rau húng, rau mùi, (Fragrant greens, mint leaves, tasty greens,)
Thì là, cải cúc, đủ loài hành hoa. (Dills, crown daisies, and all kinds of onions.)
Mồng tơi, mướp đắng, ớt cà, (Vine spinach, bitter melon, red pepper, and tomatoes,)
Bí đao đậu ván vốn nhà trồng nên. (Quash, broad beans, all are home-grown.)

In terms of botanical classification, the greens can belong to **leaf vegetable crops** (rau ăn lá), **fruit vegetable crops** (rau ăn quả), and **root vegetable crops** (rau ăn củ).

Leaf vegetable crops: water lily (rau muống, *Ipomea aquatica*), spinach (rau dền), jute leaves (rau đay), lettuce (rau diếp, rau xà lách, *Lactuca sativa*) with different kinds (leaf lettuce, butter lettuce, romaine lettuce), mustard greens (cải bẹ, *Brassica campestris*), bok choy (cải thìa, *Brassica sinensis*), cabbage (cải bắp, bắp cải, bắp su, *Brassica oleracea*), crown daisies (cải tần ô, cải cúc, *Chrysanthemum coronariumc*), vine spinach (mồng tơi, *Basella rubra*), being a vine, and, thus, is grown on the fence surrounding the house:

Nhà nàng ở cạnh nhà tôi (Her house is next to my hous)
Cách nhau một giậu **mồng tơi** *xanh rờn* (Separated by only a hedge of green vine spinach)
Hai người sống giữa cô đơn (Two persons both live in solitude)
Nàng như cũng có nỗi buồn như tôi (Looks like she has some sad story like me)
(thơ Nguyễn Bính) (Poem by Nguyễn Bính)

Water spinach (rau muống, *Ipomoea aquatica*) is present in ponds of almost all villages, especially in North Vietnam, and in folk poesy:

Anh đi anh nhớ quê nhà, (After leaving home I miss my homeland,)
Nhớ canh rau muống, nhớ cà dầm tương. (Missing water spinach soup, missing garden eggs mixed in Soy paste.)

Fruit vegetable crops: In ordinary people's thoughts, fruit are usually sweet and used for dessert, while greens are used in meals, but in botanical terms, fruit are the results of pollination and there are granules in fruit: tomatoes (*Lycopersicon esculentum*), red peppers (*Capsicum annuum*), cucumbers (*Cucumis sativus*); melon (*Cucumis melo*), zucchini (*Cucurbita pepo*); watermelon (*Citrullus landaus*); okra (*Abelmoschus esculentus*), pumpkins (*Cucurbita pepo* or *Cucurbita maxima*), edible for both the fruit and the young tops; its seeds can be fried and eaten.

Râu tôm nấu với ruột **bầu** (Shrimp feelers cooked with squash flesh,)
Chồng chan vợ húp gật đầu khen ngon. (Husband taking a spoon, wife taking a sip, both nodding and praising: it's delicious.)

Eggplant (*Solanum melongena*), is also a species of fruit vegetable crops:

Bồng em đi dạo vườn **cà** (Carrying a young brother in your arms, you walk around the **eggplant** vegetable garden,)
Trái non bỏ mắm, trái già làm dưa (The young ones you put together with fermented salted fish, the old ones, you will pickle)
Làm dưa ba bữa dưa chua (After three days, they become pickled)
Để dành ăn cấy, khỏi mua tốn tiền (Keeping them to eat, you don't need to spend money buying.)

Sponge gourd (mướp): there are many kinds, such as large gourd (mướp hương, *Luffa acutangula*), bitter gourd (mướp đắng, *Momordica charantia*), mướp ta (*Luffa cylindrica*), edible when still young, giving fibers to clean kitchenware when too old. The gourd (bầu, *Lagenaria vulgaris*) grown around the house garden, climbing in frame, giving edible fruit when still young. Squash (bí đao, *Benincasa cerifera*), grown for its fruit that can be used to make sweets.

In his poem «A Friend Coming for a Visit,» the famous poet Nguyễn Khuyến gave a sketchy description of a house garden in North Vietnam as follows:

Ao sâu nước cả, khôn chài cá, (The pond is deep, and the body of water is so large that it's difficult to fish,)
Vườn rộng rào thưa khó đuổi gà. (The garden is too large, the fence is too thin, and thus, it's difficult to chase and catch a chicken.)
Cải chửa ra hoa, **cà** *chửa nụ,* (The mustard greens have not blossomed yet, and the eggplants with no buds yet,)
Bầu vừa rụng rốn, **mướp** *đương hoa.* (The gourd has just lost its navel, and the sponge gourd has just started to blossom.)

Garden eggs and water spinach are very common and popular in North Vietnam, and are frequently met in folk poetry:

Anh đi anh nhớ quê nhà, (After leaving home I miss my homeland,)
Nhớ canh **rau muống***, nhớ* **cà** *dầm tương.* (Missing **water spinach** soup, missing **garden eggs** mixed in Soy paste.)

Root vegetable crops: like carrots, beet, radishes, kohlrabis, tomatos, etc.

Plants producing spices like ginger (*Zingiber officinale*), red pepper (*Capsicum annuum*), black pepper (*Piper nigrum*), onion, garlic, lemon grass, coriander, cinnamon leaves, laksa leaves (*Polygonum odoratum*), fish mint, mint leaves, rau thơm or húng Láng (*Mentha aquatica*), cilantro (*Limnophila aromatic*)

Ai ơi chua ngọt đã từng, (Who has sweet and sour experiences,)
Gừng *cay muối mặn xin đừng quên nhau.* (Knowing hot ginger and salty salt, please don't forget each other.)
Ớt *nào là ớt chẳng cay,* (No red pepper is not hot,)
Gái nào là gái chẳng hay ghen chồng. (No woman is not jealous about her husband.)
*Ăn tiêu nhớ **tỏi** bùi ngùi,* (You taste black pepper and, in sadness, you remember garlic,)
*Ngồi bên đám **hẹ** nhớ mùi **rau răm**,* (You look at that bunch of chives and you remember the fragrance of laksa leaves.)
Hỡi người quân tử trăm năm, (Hey ! Gentleman of hundred years,)
Quay tơ có nhớ mối tằm hay không ? (While spinning silk, do you remember the silkworm cocoon?)

Trees are also present in poetry, music, folk poetry … from the star fruit tree, the mango tree, the areca tree, the longan tree, etc.

Trees giving edible like orange, tangrines, lemons, grapefruit.

*Thân em như thể trái **chanh**,* (My body is like the lemon,)
Lắt lẻo trên cành lắm kẻ ước mơ. (Hanging loosely on the branch, making many guys to dream of.)

The boy was lamenting, not knowing if the girl had any interest in him through this poem:

*Đầu năm ăn quả **thanh yên**,* (At the begining of the year, eating a **lemon**,)
*Cuối năm ăn **bưởi** cho nên đèo bòng.* (At year's end, eating a grapefruit, and starting the dream.)

*Vì **cam** cho **quýt** đèo bòng,* (Because **orange** lets **tangerine** dreaming,)
Vì ai nhan sắc cho lòng nhớ thương. (Your beauty is causing my remembrance and my love.)

Buddha's hand (phật thủ, *Citrus medica* var. *sarcodactylis*) is a kind of fruit-producing tree that belongs to the organe / lemon family. The name of this tree comes from the form of its fruit looking like the hand of Buddha.

The Buddha's hand tree is a small tree, 2 to 2.5 m high, has flowers and fruit all year round. The Buddha's hand fruit can be eaten fresh, or used to make sweets. This kind of fruit is often part of the five-fruit tray on the Vietnamese ancestral altar during Tết Holiday. The Buddha's hand fruit is considered as the Buddha's hand, and, thus, is believed to bring peace, prosperity to the homeowners. Because of this concept and belief, many people buy this fruit and display on the altar with the expectation for good fortune, and, therefore, this fruit has become very popular.

▪ Grapefruit tree

The grapefruit is also present in folk poetry:

*Trèo lên **cây bưởi** hái hoa* (Climbing up the grapefruit tree to pick its flowers)
Bước xuống vườn cà hái nụ tầm xuân (Stepping down into the eggplant garden to pick a spring bud.)
Nụ tầm xuân nở ra xanh biếc (The spring bud is now wide open with its shining greenness)
Em lấy chồng anh tiếc lắm thay (But you are already married and I have a huge deep sorrow.)

▪ Starfruit tree

The starfruit tree is closely attached to the old house, with the yard in the back and the pond in the front, where the children play, climb and pick everyday, and also where a lot of beautiful memories are dearly kept like in this poem by Đinh Hùng:

*Độ em còn trèo **cây khế*** (At that time, you still climbed up the starfruit tree,)
Vin hái quả xanh bên tường (Anh picked the green fruit close to the wall)
Có phải chúng mình còn bé (Both of use were still very young, weren't we?)
Cho nên đời rất thơm hương? (And, therefore, our lives were nicely blessed with all fragrances?)
(thơ Đinh Hùng) (Poem by Đinh Hùng)

▪ Mango tree

The mango tree also reminds people of their house garden in the countryside:

*Quả **xoài** xưa mẹ thích,* (That mango Mother used to like,)
Cứ gợi mãi trong con; (Has always been in my mind;)
Cái hương thơm chin núc, (It was so fragrant when it was ripening,)
Cái quả bé tròn tròn; (That fruit was so small;)
*Khi cây **xoài** trước ngõ,* (When the mango tree in front of our house,)
Lấp ló trái vàng hoe, (Showing its fruit all yellow,)
Đủ nhắc cho con nhớ, (That's enough to remind me,)
Mùa hạ đã gần về. (The summer is already approaching.)
(Thanh Nguyên) (Poem by Thanh Nguyên)

▪ Lychee tree

*Mùa **vải** năm nay chừng đến muộn,* (This year, the lychee season seems to come a bit late,)
Chưa nghe tu hú giục xuân đi. (The Asian koe has not chirped to signal the end of spring.)
Nóng lòng cây gạo lìa hoa đỏ, (Getting impatient, the bombax ceiba lets its red flowers fall down,)
Trổ búp tơ xanh đón gió hè. (Its fresh green buds are open, welcoming the summer winds.)
(thơ *Nguyễn Bính*) (Poem by Nguyễn Bính)

▪ Medicinal plants

There are uncountable medicinal plants in nature. In the old days, oriental medicine used only drugs coming from plants, such as, ginger, garlic, artichoke, hibiscus leaves, fragrant greens, etc. to treat diseases. Today, even in western pharmacies, we can find several drugs made from tree leaves, roots, barks, flowers of many kinds of plants and used to treat diseases like cold, flu, arthritis, diabetes, etc. In the past, people used many chemical products but today they finally realize that chemicals have led to secondary reactions that are harmful for health, and, therefore, people pay more and more attention to biological techniques, such as: biocosmetics with may cosmetic companies are now using vegetal oils to produce powders, lipsticks, perfumes, etc.; bio mediation using vegetal organisms or microorganisms for environmental remediation.

▪ Sexual life of plants

In the animal world, the sexuality is quite simple: we have the man, the woman, the male, the female, etc. while in the plant world, the sexuality can be a bit more complex because of the following factors:

- There are trees that have only male flowers, or only have female flowers on a different trump. For example: (the ginkgo), the Actinidia (producing kiwis), the palm tree (giving dates), the papaya tree. When people grow these mono-gender trees they have to grow always both the male and the female trees in the same place or order to obtain fruit.
It is also possible that the male and female flowers are not ripening at the same time, and, therefore, the female flowers will need the powder from the male flowers for their self-fertilization. For example: the walnut tree. In biology, this phenomenon is called dichogamy.
- There are plants having separated male and female flowers but on the same trunk. For example: corn, wheat…
- There are trees or plants with flowers having both male and female pistils, such as, roses, sunflowers. These trees or

plants are called hermaphroditic. The male flowers are full of powders; the female flowers carry eggs. Thanks to winds, bees, butterflies, flower powders are carried and spread on the heads of the pistils; the powder grains sprout and get to the ovary; they touch the eggs and create the seed.

▪ Respiration and photosynthesis of plants

In biosphere, the gaseous substances like carbon, nitrogen, oxygen exist in large quantities. The other substances like phosphorus, calcium, potassium also exist but in much smaller quantities. All of these substances are needed for life. In the ecosystem, these substances are transformed from inorganic state to organic state and them back to inorganic state. Life is also dependent on the sun. The photosynthesis phenomenon transforms the light into chemical chi with the creation of glucose and oxygen. Thanks to glucose, many living organisms possess the chi that helps the respiration of plant cells.

In their respiration, the stoma of the leaves suck oxygen from the outside into the body, transform glucose and starch into chi and exhale the carbon dioxide to the outside.:

$$C_6H_{12}O_6 + 6O_2 \longrightarrow 6CO_2 + 6H_2O + \text{chemical chi}$$

The created chi helps the activities of the trees, such as, sucking of nourishing substances, water in order to assist the development of the trees, their blossoming and having fruit. The created carbon dioxide will be sucked in again to assist the process of photosynthesis for the production of glucose and starch:

$$6CO_2 + 6H_2O + \text{solar chi} \longrightarrow C_6H_{12}O_6 + 6O_2$$

The two processes of respiration and photosynthesis happened in parallel during the day; at night there is only respiration, no photosynthesis.

Therefore, there are two groups of trees:

• the group of day trees having both respiration and photosynthesis, with respiration only at night. Therefore, the efficiency rate of photosynthesis is quite low because of the compensation for respiration. This is the C3 group.
• the group of day trees having only photosynthesis with very little respiration in daylight. In this group, the efficiency rate of photosynthesis is quite high, and, therefore, the rate of dried substance / hectare is also higher. This is the C1 group. For example: corn, sugar cane.

Bibliography
Vietnamese language books

- HUỲNH QUỐC THẮNG, Lễ hội dân gian của người Việt ở Nam Bộ, NXB Văn Hóa-Thông Tin. Hà Nội, 2003
- PHAN KẾ BÍNH, Việt Nam phong tục, Khai Trí XB (Trích Đông Dương Tạp Chí từ số 24 đến 49), Sài Gòn (không đề năm)
- NGUYEN HUY, Âm Dương Ẩm Thực, TT Seattle xuất bản, Hoa Kỳ, 2016
- TOAN ANH, Nếp cũ Hội hè đình đám, quyển thượng, Sài Gòn 1969, quyển hạ, Sài Gòn, 1974
- TÂM DIỆU, Quan điểm về ăn chay của Đạo Phật, Hoa sen xb, Hoa Kỳ, 2009
- THUẦN ĐỨC, Ăn chay, Saigon, 1928
- TRẦN ANH KIỆT, Ăn chay và sức khỏe, Úc Châu, 2000

Foreign language books

- CARPER, Jean, les aliments et leur vertu, Les Éditions de l'homme, Québec, 1994
- CASTLEMAN, Michael, Les plantes qui guérissent, Mordu Vivendi, Canada, 2002
- CHEE Soo, Le Tao de la longue vie, un guide pratique de l'alimentation Ch'ang Ming, 1983, Éd. Le Jour, Montréal,
- CHEN Jun et Pierre Sterckx, Diététique des quatre saisons, Presses universitaires Quang Ming, Suisse 2002.
- CHEN, You Wa, La diététique du yin et du yang, Éd. Robert Laffont, Paris, 1995
- EYSSALET, J.M. Guillaume, G. et al. Diététique énergétique et médecine chinoise, Éd. Présence, France, 1984
- LACASSE, Odette, Plantes médicinales et aromatiques de nos jardins, Broquet, Canada, 1994
- OSSIPOW, Laurence, Le végétalisme: vers un autre art de vivre, Paris Montréal, Cerf Fides, 1989
- MERRY, André, Les végétariens: raison et sentiments, Paris, La Plage éd, 1998
- NGUYEN VAN NGHI, Hoang Ti Nei King So Quenn, 4 tomes, Socedim, Marseille, 1973 et 1991
- NGUYEN VAN NGHI, TRAN V.D. et C. NGUYEN Recours, Huang Di Nei Jing, Ling Shu, 3 tomes, Marseille, 1994, 1995, 1999
- OHSAWA, Georges, Le zen macrobiotique, Librairie philo. J. Vrin, Paris, 1980
- Sélection du Reader's Digest, — Secrets et vertus des plantes médicinales, 1er Édit. Canadienne, 1991
- — Aliments santé, Aliments danger, Canada, 1997
- SIONNEAU, Philippe et Zagorski, Richard, La diététique du Tao, Éd. Guy Trédaniel, Paris, 2001
- TREMBLAY, Nicole, Le Tao de l'alimentation, Les Éditions Québécor, Canada, 2002

Introducing books available on Amazon

Mục lục, Dẫn nhập Bài 1. Khái niệm văn hóa, **Phần 1.** *Văn hóa thời Hùng Vương,* Bài 2. Văn Lang-Âu Lạc, Bài 3. Cái váy, Bài 4. Đôi đũa, Bài 5. Chó đá linh thiêng, Bài 6. Trầu cau. **Phần 2.** *Hình thành văn hóa Đại Việt,* Bài 7. Bối cảnh thời Bắc thuộc, Bài 8. Sáng tạo tiếng Hán Việt, Bài 9. Áo yếm, **Phần 3.** *Bối cảnh Viễn Đông,* Bài 10. Đình làng, Bài 11. Cơm làng, Bài 12. Linh hồn con nghê, Bài 13. Thăng Long, Bài 14. Cây nêu, Bài 15. Tết, Bài 16. Bàn thờ tổ tiên, Bài 17. Vái lạy, Bài 18. Cơm Tết, **Phần 4.** *Trung tâm văn hóa Huế,* Bài 19. Huế, Bài 20. Triết lý giáo dục vua Nguyễn, Bài 21. Ngự thiện, Bài 22. Nguồn gốc áo dài, Bài 23. Nón lá, Bài 24. Văn hóa của căn nhà, Bài 25. Cây kiểng,**Thư tịch**

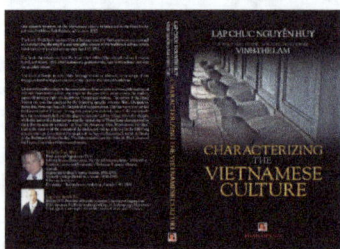

1. The Concept of Culture, **Part 1. Culture of the Hùng Vương Era,** 2. Southeast Asian Culture, 3. The Story of Betel and areca, 4. Skirt of Hùng Vương era, 5. The chopsticks culture, 6. The Sacred Stone Dog, **Part 2. Formation of Great Viet culture,** 7. Chinese Domination Era, 8. Yếm, **Part 3. Far Eastern Field,** 9. The village community hall, 10. Village banquets, 11. The Soul of Nghê, 12. Thăng Long, 3. The Tết Pole, 14 Origin of Tết, 15. Tết Meal, 16. The ancestral altar, **Part 4. Cultural centre Huế,** 17. Huế, 18. Educational philosophy, 19. Royal Meal, 20. Áo dài, 21. Nón lá, 22. The culture in traditional house. 23. Cây Kiểng

Mục Lục, Lời nói đầu, **Chương 1. Văn hóa XHCN và sáng tác,** *Chuyện lạ về lãng mạn ..., Chuyện lạ về thơ tình cảm, Chuyện lạ về « Chàng Thơ » ,Chuyện lạ về ca dao ,Chuyện lạ về tà áo* ,**Chương 2. Văn hóa XHCN và giáo dục** *Chuyện lạ về kỹ sư tâm hồn,Chuyện lạ về gương anh hùng,* **Chương 3. Văn hóa XHCN và lịch sử,** *Chuyện lạ về dâng đất, Chuyện lạ về người đã chết,* **Chương 4. Văn hóa XHCN và tín ngưỡng,** *Chuyện lạ về Đền Hồ, Chuyện lạ về vong hồn của Bác, Chuyện lạ về "ước mơ "của Bác, Chuyện lạ về Ông Trời,* **Chương 5. Văn hóa và kinh tế,** *Chuyện lạ về đạo đức, Chuyện lạ về giết cha, Chuyện lạ về người đầy tớ, Chuyện lạ về giấc mơ*

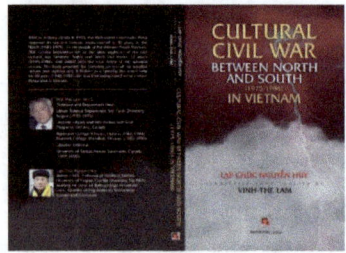

Part 1. *Socialist Culture: Cultural and educational theories,* **1. Theoretical foundation,** Hồ Chí Minh, Trường Chinh, **2. Creation of intangible culture,** Textual literature Poetry and music in the socialist culture, Folk literature, Nhân văn giai phẩm Group, **3. Socialist education,** Theory of socialist education, Leadership training, Soul engineer, **4. Historical role,** Propaganda needs, Serving politics, *Part 2.* Socialist culture: *Infrastructure building,* **5. Socialist infrastructure,** Co-operatives, GBS (Government-based supply regime GBS), Family registry regime, Stamp/fiche regime, 6. Image of a dreamed society, Documents from the period of government-based organization of GBS, Ordinary daily life, *Part 3. Socialist culture:* Collapse, **7. Northern battlefront,** Abolition of the old culture, Return to the old culture, Changes in the countryside, **8. Civil war « on Paper »,** Book burning and writer's arrest, Activation of cultural laws Saigon's cultural victory, **9. Civil war "in Sound",** Types of music, Burning of music and inhibition of songs, Victory of the Saigon Bolero sound,**Bibliography**

Partie 1. La culture socialiste : théories culturelles et pédagogiques, 1. Fondements théoriques, 2. Créer une culture intangible, 3. L'éducation socialiste, 4. Le rôle de l'Histoire, **Partie 2. Édifier l'infrastructure de la culture socialiste,** 5. L'infrastructure socialiste, 6. Le fantasme d'une société imaginée, **Partie 3. La culture socialiste : l'effondrement,** 7. La ligne de front du Nord, 8. Une guerre civile sur papier, *9. Une guerre civile de l'audition,* La victoire du boléro de Saigon

Phần 1. Văn hóa XHCN: *Lý thuyết văn hóa giáo dục,* 1. Cơ sở lý thuyết , 2. Sáng tạo văn hóa vô thể, 3. Giáo dục XHCN, 4. Vai trò của lịch sử, **Phần 2.** *Văn hóa XHCN : Xây dựng hạ tầng cơ sở,* 5. Hạ tầng cơ sở XHCN, 6. Từ giấc mơ đến hiện thực, **Phần 3.** *Văn hóa XHCN : Sụp đổ,* 7. Trận địa tại miền Bắc, 8. Nội chiến « *trên giấy* », 9. Nội chiến trong *"âm thanh",* Chiến thắng của âm thanh bolero Sài Gòn, **Phụ lục 1 : Nghĩa quân văn hóa Vũ Hoàng Chương, Phụ lục 2 : Nghĩa quân văn hóa Nghiêm Thẩm**

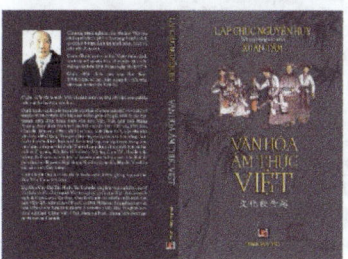

Dẫn nhập, **Phần 1. Cơm vua,** *Ngự thiện, Khí âm dương, Nhận diện Khí âm dương Khí mùi vị,* **Phần 2. Thực dụng của văn hóa ẩm thực,** *Tạng khí, Cách dùng khí ẩm thực,* **Phần 3. Ẩm thực trong thế tâm linh,** *Cơm cúng,* **Phần 4. Ẩm thực và tôn giáo,** *Cơm chay,* Phụ lục 1. Khí trái cây, Phụ lục 2. Văn hóa trong món ăn, Phụ lục 3. Cơm nhà Phụ lục 4. Đôi đũa, Phụ lục 5. Các chất phụ gia, Phụ lục 6. Yến tiệc trong cung vua triều Nguyễn, Thư mục

Introduction **Part 1. Royal Meal,** *Royal meal, Yin and yang, Identification of the food chi, The chi of flavors,* **Part 2. Practical Use of Culinary Culure,** *Chi of internal organs, Use of food chi,* **Part 3. Culinary Culture in Spiritual Life,** *worshipped meal,* **Part 4. Culinary Culture and Religion,** *Vegetarian meal,* Appendix 1. Chi in fruit, Appendix 2. Culture in meals, Appendix 3. Additives, Appendix 4. Palace feasts under Nguyễn Dynasty, Appendix 5. Vegetables in Vietnamese poetry, Bibliograpphy.

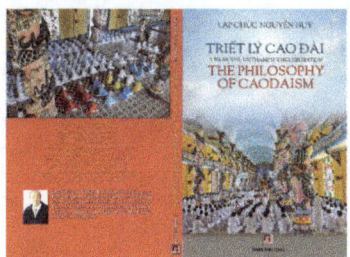

Works by Vinh-The Lam

Book to be published
Full Circle: Memoir of a Vietnamese-Canadian Librarian. London, U.K.: Austin-Macauley, 2022

Books already published
1. *ALA Từ Điển Giải Nghĩa Thư Viện Học và Tin Học Anh-Việt*. Tucson, Arizona: Galen Press, 1996. (Translation: original English title: *ALA Glossary of Library and Information Science*, edited by Heartsill Young; co-translators: Phạm Thị Lệ-Hương, and Nguyễn Thị Nga).
2. *Bộ Quy Tắc Biên Mục Anh-Mỹ Rút Gọn, 1988*. Virgia, U.S.: LEAF-VN (Library and Education Assistance Foundation for Vietnam), 2002 (Translation: original English title: *The Concise AACR2, 1988 Revision*, by Michael Gorman; co-translator: Phạm Thị Lệ-Hương).
3. *Đakao Trong Tâm Tưởng* (Đakao in my heart and my thoughts). Hamilton, Ont.: Hoài Việt, 2008.
4. *Bạch Hóa Tài Liệu Mật của Hoa Kỳ về Việt Nam Cộng Hòa* (Declassifying classified U.S. documents on the Republic of Vietnam). Hamilton, Ont.: Hoài Việt, 2008.
5. *Việt Nam Cộng Hòa, 1963-1967: Những Năm Xáo Trộn* (Republic of Vietnam, 1963-1967: years of political chaos, Vietnamese edition). Hamilton, Ont.: Hoài Việt, 2010.
6. *Republic of Vietnam, 1963-1967: Years of Political* Chaos. Hamilton, Ont.: Hoài Việt, 2010.
7. *Truy Cập Thông Tin Theo Chủ Đề (Subject Access to Information)*. Ho Chi Minh City: Saigon University, Dept. of Library and Information Science, 2010.
8. *The Price of Freedom: Exodus and Diaspora of Vietnamese People*. Westminster, Calif.: Người Việt Books, 2017 (Translation: original Vietnamese title: *Giá Tự Do* by Lâm Vĩnh Bình).
9. *Cultural Research Field Trips*. Montreal: Vietnamese Youth and College Students of Montreal, 2018 (Translation: original Vietnamese title *Du Khảo Văn Hóa*, by Lạp Chúc Nguyễn Huy).
10. *Vietnam, Territoriality, and the South China Sea: Paracel and Spratly Islands*. London, U.K.: Routledge 2019 (Translation: original Vietnamese title: *Những Bằng Chứng về Chủ Quyền của Việt Nam Đối Với Hai Quần Đảo Hoàng Sa Trường Sa*, by Hãn Nguyên Nguyễn Nhã).
11. *The History of South Vietnam: The Quest for Legitimacy and Stability, 1963-1967*. London, U.K.: Routledge, 2021.
12. *Tròn Nhiệm Vụ: Hồi Ký của một Quản Thủ Thư Viện Canada Gốc Việt* (Vietnamese edition of: *Full circle: memoir of a Vietnamese-Canadian Llibrarian*). Westminster, Calif.: Nhân Ảnh, 2021.
13. *Trường Petrus Ký Trong Tâm Tưởng: Nhớ về Trường Cũ, Thầy Cô, và Bạn Học* (Petrus Ký High School in my heart and my thoughts: remembering the old school, my teachers and my classmates). Westminster, Calif.: Nhân Ảnh, 2021.
14. *Quân Lực Việt Nam Cộng Hòa: Một Quân Đội Anh Hùng Bị Bức Tử* (Armed Forces of the Republic of Vietnam: a heroic army unjustly abandoned and left for ded, Vietnamese edition). Westminster, Calif.: Nhân Ảnh, 2021.
15. *Armed Forces of the Republic of Vietnam: A Heroic Army Unjustly Abandoned and Left for Dead*. Westminster, Calif.: Nhân Ảnh, 2022.

Research Studies
Accessible from the Translator's bilingual (Vietnamese and English) personal Website:
Tuyển tập Vĩnh Nhơn Lâm Vĩnh Thế: trang chủ (tuyen-tap-vinh-nhon-lam-vinh-the.blogspot.com)

Works by Lạp Chúc Nguyễn Huy

Books Already Published
- 2023 The Philosophy of Caodaism, A bilingual Vietnamese-English Edition, Nhân Ảnh XB
- 2023 Văn hóa ẩm thực, Nhân Ảnh XB[72]
- 2022 Nội chiến văn hóa Bắc Nam 1975-1986 trên đất Việt, Cultural Civil War Between North and South (1975-1986) In Vietnam Nhân Ảnh XB[73] ☺
- 2022 Định hình văn Việt (Characterizing the Vietnamese culture), Nhân Ảnh published[74].
- 2022 Chuyện lạ nước Việt (Strange stories of Vietnam), Nhân Ảnh published.
- 2019 Lịch sử Hội Thánh Em, Liên Hiệp Hội Thánh Em (History of the Younger Brother Church), Federation of Younger Brother Church published.
- 2016 Âm Dương Ẩm Thực, (Yin-Yang eating) TT Seattle published.
- 2015 Thiên Thư Tòa Thánh (Holy Book of the Church), Caodai Research Institute published.
- 2005 Le Caodaïsme (Cao Daiism), Théorie des Trois Trésors et des Cinq Fluides (Theory of Three treasures and Five Fluids), Chân Tâm Publisher, California.
- 1995 Triết Lý Đạo Cao Đài, (Philosophy of Cao Daiism), Minh Thiện published, Canada.
- 1994 Văn Hóa Việt (Vietnamese culture), Nắng Mới published, Canada.
- 1992 Religion et adaptation: les réfugiés vietnamiens au Canada, (Religion and adaptation : the Vietnamese refugees in Canada), Université Laval, Canada. *
- 1990 Fleur de lotus et feuille d'érable, La vie religieuse des Vietnamiens du Québec, (Lotus flower and the maple leaf: the religious life of the Vietnamese of Quebec). Université Laval, March 1990*
- 1988 Exile in a cold land, a Vietnamese community in Canada, Yale Center, U.S.A. *
- 1984 Les Vietnamiens du Québec: profil sociolinguistique, (The Vietnamese of Quebec : sociolinguistic profile), Centre international de recherche sur le bilinguisme, B.136, Québec
- 1972 Hiện tình kinh tế Việt Nam, 2 tập, (Current economic situation of Vietnam, 2 Volumes), Lửa Thiêng published, Saigon.

Research Articles
- 2008 Des poids et des mesures dans les campagnes du Vietnam, (Weights and measurements in the countryside of Vietnam), École française d'Extrême-Orient, (Institut de Recherche sur le Sud-Est Asiatique, T.2, Paris*
- 1998 Le *Thờ Mẫu*, un chamanisme vietnamien? (Mẫu Cult : a Vietnamese chamanism?) Anthropologie et Société, Université Laval, Québec *
- 1993 De quelques usages du sel dans la culture vietnamienne, (Some usages of salt in
- Vietnamese culture), Collection Grand Sud Nº 4, Prince of Songkhla University, Thaïland
- 1990 Le caodaïsme, Fleur de lotus et feuille d'érable, La vie religieuse des Vietnamiens du Québec, (Caodaism, Lotus flower and maple leaf, the religious life of Vietnamese of Quebec), Univertsité Laval, March 1990*
- 1987 Les Vietnamiens à Québec et leurs problèmes d'intégration (The Vietnamese people in Quebec and their problems in adaptation), Centre international de recherche sur le bilinguisme, publication B-164, Canada *
- 1985 The survival of the Vietnamese language in Quebec, the Vietnam forum No.6, U.S.A. *
- 1974 Les marais salants de la province de Bạc Liêu, (Salt marshes of the Province of Bạc Liêu), Société des Études indochinoises, T. XLIX.
- 1968 Les formations latéritiques à Bình Dương, (Clay formations in Bình Dương), Société des Études indochinoises, T. XLIII.
- 1962 Une agglomération de sampans habités à Saigon, (An Agglomeration of habited sampans in Saigon), C.O.M., T.XV,

English-Vietnamese Bilingual E-Books
Hệ Phái Cao Đài, The Fractions of Caodaism, 278 pages, Văn hóa Cao Đài, The Culture of Caodaism, 187 pages, Lịch sử Chi Phái Quốc Doanh (History of the government-controlled fraction), 107 pages. To read E-books, please get into: daocaodai.info; wordpress.daocaodai-chauau.eu;tusachcaodai.wordpress.com; Lạp chúc nguyễn huy

* Co-author
Amazon

---

[72] Bản Anh ngữ : The Vietnamese Culinary Culture, Nhân Ảnh 2023

[73] GS Vĩnh Thế Lâm, cựu giáo sư ĐH Vạn Hạnh và University of Saskatchewan, chuyển sang anh ngữ dưới tựa đề Cultural Civil War Between North and South (1975-1986) In Vietnam, NXB Nhân Ảnh 2022
  GS Louis Jacques Dorais, professeur émérite của ĐH Laval, Canada chuyển sang pháp ngữ dưới tựa đề Guerre civile culturelle entre le Nord et le Sud au Vietnam (1975-1986), Nhân Ảnh 2023.

[74] GS Vĩnh Thế Lâm chuyển sang anh ngữ dưới tựa đề Characterizing the Vietnamese culture, Nhân Ảnh, 2022

Nhân Ảnh
2024

Liên lạc với tác giả
Lạp Chúc Nguyễn Huy 2415 Place Lafortune Ouest
ST Laurent, PQ H4M 1A7
Canada
Điện thoại: 438 386 0638
Email: nguyenhuyquebec@yahoo.ca

Liên lạc Nhà xuất bản
Nhân Ảnh
E.mail: han.le3359@gmail.com
(408) 722-5626